GLOBAL BUSINESS SERIES

Doing Business with Taiwan

Doing Business with Korea

Doing Business with Singapore

Doing Business with Thailand

Doing Business with China

Doing Business with Mexico

Doing Business
with Mexico

Paul Leppert

JAIN PUBLISHING COMPANY
Fremont, California

This book is designed to provide helpful information for people doing business with Mexico. It is sold with the understanding that it is not meant to render legal, medical, accounting, or other professional advice. For such services contact a competent practitioner. Some are listed in this book.

Library of Congress Cataloging-in-Publication Data

Leppert, Paul A.
    Doing business with Mexico / Paul Leppert.
        p.   cm. — (Global business series)
    Includes bibliographical references and index.
    ISBN 0-87573-046-9 (paper : alk. paper)
    1. Mexico—Commerce—United States. 2. United States—Commerce—Mexico. 3. Business etiquette—Mexico.
4. National characteristics, Mexican. 5. Mexico—Economic conditions—1982-
I. Title. II. Series.
HF3238.U5L47   1995
650'.0972—dc20   95-20285
                                           CIP

Contents

Introduction

With the implementation of the North American Free Trade Agreement facts long in shadow now loom in sharp profile. We see a Mexico with the world's fifteenth largest economy, fourth largest oil reserves, and eleventh largest population, over eighty-five million.

For businesses in the United States, Mexico offers abundant supplies of energy and raw materials, cheap labor, a large market of consumers, close proximity to the United States, and easy access to the rest of Latin America. Even before NAFTA, Mexico was the third largest market for U.S. exports and the fifth largest source for U.S. imports. Business opportunities abound!

But so do the risks. The ease with which citizens of the United States can enter Mexico obscures the fact that it has a vastly different culture. Doing business with Mexico may seem deceptively easy. In fact it is fraught with many problems.

Because past relations have been riddled with military conflict, economic rivalry, and social animosity, the long line dividing Mexico and the United States is more a scar than a boundary. It would be difficult to find a national border, anywhere in the world, which separates more different societies and systems. Viewed from the United States, Mexico can seem more complex than Europe, more foreign than Asia. Mexico, because of its blend of Indian and Spanish blood, is even different from the rest of Latin America, where ethnic divisions are more distinct and people of European stock often rule.

For many Americans, mention of Mexico stirs up stereotypes: mustachioed musicians under straw sombreros strumming guitars; illegal immigrants, clothes held high, wading the Rio Grande; desperadoes and donkeys, tacos and tequila, long siestas in the shade of cacti.

The situation cries out for understanding. Culture is more than cliché. It consists of values and behaviors which are deeply imprinted on hundreds of generations. In its grasp we are all Pavlovian dogs.

Mexican culture, derived from both Spanish and Indian heritages, stresses a rigid personal dignity, a fondness for fatalism, rule by men rather than law, male machismo, and sharp distinctions between social classes. These contrast with the culture of the United States which emphasizes informality, sexual and social equality, individual responsibility, civil liberties, free enterprise and the rule of law. Though neither culture completely lives up to its standards, the differences create profound problems for personal and business interaction. Indeed, it is not possible to do business with Mexicans successfully without first understanding their culture.

The first part of this book describes cultural and social factors which affect doing business in Mexico. Culture, a product of history, is passed from generation to generation by such institutions as the family and school. The business behavior of your Mexican counterpart will be profoundly affected by the culture he or she learned as a child. To do business with Mexicans you must learn how Mexican culture affects Mexican behavior.

The second part of this book deals with the economic and business environment in Mexico. It explains how the Mexican economy and business system originated and developed and describes its successes, opportunities, problems, and pitfalls. Of particular interest are Mexico's business procedures, bargaining techniques, and sources of help. These too, are rooted in culture.

The third and final section is concerned with your personal experience with Mexico: travel tips; things to do, see, and learn; living conditions, useful addresses, and recommended reading. Your business in Mexico will be better if you make a good personal adjustment and enjoy your experience.

This book is based partly on interviews with Mexican and U.S. business people and government officials. It is designed to get you started. It does not pretend to provide legal advice or solutions to specific business problems which vary widely. Conditions in Mexico are constantly changing. There are new regulations almost daily. Although every effort has been made to ensure accuracy there are always exceptions such as local rules and alternative procedures. Much will depend upon how well you bargain. Be sure to check the offices and agencies in chapters nine and thirteen for the latest information before making business decisions.

The information provided here does not represent the views of any agencies of the governments of Mexico or the United States. Money is denominated in U.S. dollars unless otherwise specified.

PART ONE

Knowing Your Counterpart

Mexicans have different business goals and procedures from ours because their culture holds different values. To understand these people we need to know how they view themselves, their families, society, work, culture, and politics.

Your Mexican counterpart will act and react according to cultural patterns established in childhood. These indelible imprints, like the delicately etched circuits of computer chips, program both social and business behavior.

If you understand your Mexican counterpart's cultural conditioning, you will go into a business situation with a decided advantage. To a certain extent you will be able to predict his or her behavior.

Understanding another culture with its vast, complicated currents is not easy. It requires a study, not only of the past from which a culture originates, but of the institutions which pass it to new generations.

The benefits from taking the time and effort to learn about Mexican culture are many. In addition to obtaining a business advantage you will receive, as a bonus, a new understanding of your own culture. Your perspective on life will never be quite the same.

1. Culture and Society

The Land

The land of Mexico is more diverse than some continents. There is an emptiness to its dry northern landscape. The desert displays a desolate and barren beauty. The wind, whistling between the hills, blows wheels of sage brush before it. At dusk distant mountains cast dark shadows down dusty canyons.

Mexico is dominated by a rugged central plateau, the Meseta Central, which is bordered by mountain ranges. At the southern edge of the plateau, nestled in a valley, sits Mexico City. In the south the Isthmus of Tehuantepec, only 150 miles wide, separates the Pacific Ocean from the Gulf of Mexico. Two peninsulas complete the country: the long, narrow Baja in the northwest and the Yucatán in the southeast.

Rainfall patterns have had a profound effect on Mexico's culture and economy. Though the southern half of Mexico is in the tropics, altitude is more important than latitude. Mountains block many rain clouds, making the central plateau a desert of cactus, sage, and mesquite. Here rain, which falls between June and September, is spasmodic and capricious. In the lowlands of the Yucatán rain soaks so quickly through porous limestone soils that little is left for use.

To avoid famine the ancient Toltecs, Aztecs, and Mayans propitiated the rain gods with human sacrifices. Unfortunately, the gods have short memories. Today lack of rain is a major factor in Mexico's need to import much of its food.

The Indians

Mexico has more Indian influence, by blood and culture, than any other nation in the Western Hemisphere. On the U.S. frontier Indians were exterminated; in Mexico they were accepted as spouses and lovers. Most modern Mexicans are *mestizos*, mixtures of Indian and Spanish ancestry. In the south there are still many pureblood Indians.

About forty thousand years ago nomadic Asian tribes crossed to America over a land bridge created when an ice age lowered the level of the Bering Sea. These first Americans, like later immigrants, came for economic reasons: to be the first to exploit a new land filled with fish and game. In this hunter's paradise they followed the mammoth, killed it, and drove it to extinction. As the ice age ended, warm rain turned the valley of Mexico into a large lake. Along the marshy shore large animals, mired in the mud, were easy game.

Ironically, a long drought brought agriculture. As vegetation became sparse game disappeared. The Indians, driven by hunger, tried to eat wild plants. One, maize, yielded kernels which became cornmeal when ground between stones. When flattened and baked the meal became a delicious wrapper for meat, vegetables, or sauces. Corn could be cultivated almost anywhere.

By the time the rains returned corn, beans, and squash had become staples. With the addition of livestock, the Indians now had a secure source of food. They could now live in one place and had time to develop skills such as weaving and pottery. Mexican culture had begun.

Mexico's first creations from clay symbolized the mystery of fertility. These were renditions of naked women with fine-featured faces and fully-formed figures. Some ceramics depicted dwarfs and hunchbacks, establishing a tradition of obsession with the bizarre. In time the Aztecs built zoos to display deformed people and the Mayans carved figures of freaks (considered supernatural) out of stone. Some Mexicans still check their new-born babies to make sure all their parts are human.

Mexico's ancient Indians lived in a world of inexplicable enchantment, filled with shamans, secret sorcery, corn gods, ritual masks, and magic trances. Yet they produced practical civilizations. The Mayans, skilled in the arts and sciences, became the Greeks of Mexico; the Aztecs, experts at power, the Romans. So accurate was the astronomy of the Mayan priests that they calculated the orbit of Venus within a few seconds and created the best calendar of their time, one designed to pick the most appropriate days for planting and harvesting crops.

The priests took their rewards by requiring commoners to build them great stone edifices: mansions, pyramids, palaces, temples, and observatories. Here, in the inner cities, they lived in luxury while the common folk were restricted to suburban slums. These people provided the farming, hunting, and handicrafts for the inner city but they were allowed in it only for special religious and market days.

Today the Indian imprint on Mexico is indelible. It permeates daily life and is chiseled into the features of the *mestizo*.

Religion

The Indian was deeply rooted in nature. Life was a magic moment in time and space in which all things were perfect and immediate. The senses communed with a world that was holy. The Indian knew, with deep certitude, the need for human sacrifice to sustain the sanctity, beauty, and order of this marvelous universe. For the Indian religion the sacrifice of humans ensured the salvation of a world which was good. In contrast Christianity requires the death of a god/man to save humanity from a world which is evil.

High mounds were built so worshipers could view this ritual. In time they became immense soaring structures, big blocks of rock. Each pyramid was dedicated to a particular deity. The lifeblood of the victims flowed from the top, sustaining creation. Those who died on the pyramids reappeared in the harvests, mimicking a natural order in which every sunset was a sacrificial death; every sunrise, a resurrection.

For the ancient Indians the sacrament of human sacrifice possessed a beauty, blessedness, and tenderness which can only be described in poetry:

> Come sweet child, time for planting
> With garlands, bleed and burn
> Huge harvests!
> Genealogy of the gods!
> All life is life after death.

Before we judge this practice we should consider the prevalence of human sacrifice in major world religions. It was practiced in Judea until God allowed Abraham to substitute a ram for his son. Christianity extended it to the ritual sacrifice of a god/man. Circumcision is a vestige of human sacrifice which is based on the hope God will accept a part in place of the whole person.

With the Spanish conquest of Mexico the Indians lost their gods, temples, and independence. They became beasts of labor in mines and fields, seekers of relief from poverty, misery, and humiliation. The despair of the Indians endangered the Spanish because it could lead to rebellion. So the Spanish offered the Indians succor in the form of medieval Catholicism. The Indians, long accustomed to seeing men sacrificed to gods, were given a god who sacrificed himself for man. To be accepted Jesus had to experience suffering greater than the Indians', which was considerable. They would have no use for a god who endured plain, ordinary human torments. So the Spanish clergy went out of its way to make the suffering of Christ impressive. This led to the standard Mexican crucifix which depicts a bleeding Jesus, ribs protruding, writhing in grotesque agony. It magnified the brooding, mystical torment of the Indians while reflecting their anguish and humiliation. The divinity of Jesus became credible to the Indians because his suffering was incredible.

Additional steps were taken to Indianize Christianity. Shortly after the Spanish conquest the Virgin of Guadalupe miraculously appeared to Juan Diego, an Indian boy. The apparition took place on a site once devoted to a shrine to the Aztec goddess of fertility. The miracle took place on an Aztec holy day. Nevertheless the Spanish Church canonized the Virgin. She became the consoling mother of Mexico. Her likeness is found in plush corporate offices and humble homes in the poorest slums. Mexicans still throng to the site of the vision, a hillock on the north side of Mexico City.

Other factors smoothed the transition of faiths. There were many similarities between the Indian religions and Spanish Catholicism. Both crafted statues of their gods, saints and idols. Both shared sacraments of baptism, communion, and confession. The Aztecs chewed pieces of figurines of the god Huitzilopochtli, made of ground amaranth seeds and the blood of boys; the Catholic consumed the body and blood of Christ in Communion. Both burned incense and candles.

When the Spanish destroyed Aztec and Mayan temples they often built Catholic cathedrals on the same sites. These locations were already sacred to the Indians because they were venues of ancient supernatural events or the abodes of nature spirits. Many Indian gods were reincarnated as Catholic saints: the Aztec god of harvest became San Isidro; the rain god, San Sebastian. Significant vestiges of the Indian religions were tolerated. In the Yucatán religious ceremonies still include the ritual trances of the ancient Mayans.

Modern Mexico is supposed to be secular. Mass attendance and ordination of priests is declining. Birth control and divorce are common. Abortion, though illegal, is practiced by many poor. Yet ninety-three per cent of Mexicans are nominally Catholic.

Catholic or Indian, nominal or real, religion seems to permeate daily life. When surprised, scared, or overwrought Mexicans exclaim the names of God, Jesus, and Mary. They display religious artifacts and pictures of the Virgin of Guadalupe. Their amulets, Christian and Indian, range from crucifixes to necklaces of garlic. Some are modern. In the Yucatán my bus driver had two talismans hanging over his windshield: Jesus on the Cross and Yogi Bear on skateboards. Somehow there was always room when our bus passed cars on winding one-lane roads. Once, at high speed, we hit a truck. Miraculously, we kept going.

The Indians appear to accept Catholicism. Some walk miles on bloody knees to beg God's favors at cathedrals. A few on Christian holy days lug crosses up the sides of volcanoes. But one senses that deep down their inner natures remain inviolable, still Indian, mystical and unfathomable, heeding the ancient magic of the shamans.

In the Mayan sacrificial rite eight slaves had their throats slit and the heart was torn out of a virgin. The victims were told they were performing a community service and would return as parrots or monkeys. Unlike the Aztecs the Mayans did not eat portions of their victims. The Mayan practice of drowning virgins at the time of planting was practiced in some villages up to the early twentieth century when it was discontinued due to a shortage of virgins.

Aztec sacrifice differed from Mayan. In the standard ritual four acolytes held the victim's limbs while a priest with an obsidian knife cut deftly under the ribs, excised the heart, and held it high. When done with the right aplomb the pulsating heart gushed fountains of consecrated blood. The procedure varied according to the god being worshiped. When sacrificing a particularly brave warrior to Hummingbird, the god of war, Aztec priests would eat part of the victim's flesh to transfer courage. According to Will Durant such ritual cannibalism was once almost universal. Symbolic vestiges remain in many modern religions such as Christian Communion. Aztec victims for the god of rain were bound and pierced with arrows. Their blood drops sprinkling the soil symbolized rain. Sacrifices to the fire god were cremated while alive.

The gods of rain, corn, and war were insatiable. Though long lines of victims climbed the pyramids there were never enough to go around. Few people volunteered to be victims as long as others were available. So constant war was waged to obtain captives for sacrifice. Priests used astronomy to ensure the right victims were sacrificed at the right times. It was a brutal system which integrated science, war, agriculture, and religion. The horror fed on itself. It left a legacy for modern Mexico: fascination with blood and death.

The Conquest

José Vasconcelos, the founder of modern Mexican education, defined Mexican culture as "Castilian and Moorish, with Aztec markings." Thus he emphasized the importance of both the Spanish conquest of Mexico and the earlier Moorish conquest of Spain.

Invasion was nothing new to the Indians of Central Mexico. They were frequently invaded by hordes of nomadic warriors from the northwest. One such incursion was led by Mixcoatl, a sort of Indian Genghis Khan.

By the time Cortés and his small band assailed Mexico, the Aztec civilization was old and declining. It was vulnerable to a tiny army consisting, not of professionals, but of soldiers of fortune who fought for booty, slaves, and women. They had superior military technology consisting of steel swords, armor, and horses. Cortés won Mexico through a combination of power, luck, deceit, and cruelty. He was a stickler for detail. He tried to extract the location of hidden Indian treasures from Aztec nobles by holding their feet over a fire. But first he made sure they were well oiled.

The confrontation between Indian and Spaniard was fraught with misunderstandings. The Aztec leader Montezuma at first thought Cortés was an ancient god Quetzalcoatl returning from self-imposed exile. So said the omens and portents. Even after this illusion cleared the Aztecs had difficulty 'making sense of Cortés, especially his circus-like entourage of falcons, jesters, tumblers, and jugglers. The Spanish, knowing nothing of tobacco, saw smoke spouting from the mouths of Indians and considered it a trick of the devil. There were also language difficulties. A Spaniard exploring the east coast of Mexico asked some local Mayans the name of their peninsula. They replied "*ci-u-than*," so the Spaniard named the area *Yu-ca-tan*, the closest sound in Spanish. *Ci-u-than* in Mayan means "We don't understand you."

For the Indian the psychological impact of the Conquest was devastating. In a few years his ancient culture was swept away. His women betrayed him for the Spaniards. Some were raped by the conquerors. The result was a mixed race, *mestizo*, which was insecure about its origins and identity. It could criticize the conquistadors only by rejecting its own bloodlines.

The Spanish legacy to Mexico is both ambivalent and enduring. In all of Mexico there are no statues to Cortés. Yet the nation speaks his language and practices his religion. Mexico is thickly encrusted with the residue of sixteenth century Spain: baroque churches, bullrings, and village dignitaries dressed in colonial clothes.

Machismo, Mañana, Ahora

Mexico's ancient Indian cultures centered on male role-models: shamans, priests and warriors. The culture of the Spanish conquerors had been conditioned by eight centuries of occupation by the Moors who regarded women as inferior. So it is no wonder that Mexican society is dominated by males. Sex roles are sharply defined. Male values are summarized as *machismo*, emphasizing courage, strength, manly dignity, and sexual ability.

Often the need to appear *macho* leads to bravado, braggadocio, bluffing, and posturing. Neurotic needs to prove oneself a man can surface in many ways: the fatalism of the matador, the studied nonchalance of the bus driver speeding around blind curves as bald tires slip on muddy mountain roads, the prickly cactus-like defensiveness of the Mexican drunk, the brutality of the wife beater, and the flowery but insidious comments Mexican men strew in the paths of lone women.

Mexican *machismo* is exhibited in the bullring, where the adoration of blood and death derived from the Aztecs, Mayans, and Spanish receive full play. The bullfight recreates a religious ritual as old as ancient Crete: slaying of a sacred animal in violent vespers. The lances of the picadors, like the slings and arrows of life, make the bull more miserable than he would otherwise be. Blood streams from his neck wounds. The matador, *machismo* incarnate, challenges the looming black hulk in a glittering costume of gold and red. As dusk draws near the drama unfolds, a dance of sun and shade, light and shadow, dust and death. Nearly always fate decrees the death of the bull.

The fatalism of the bullring extends to everyday life. Most Mexicans feel more like the bull than the matador. If one cannot shape one's future, why not delay duties and unpleasantries and enjoy the present? So responsibilities are often put off until *mañana*, not just tomorrow but all the tomorrows to come. Pleasures, in contrast, are taken *ahora*, now. This stress on immediate gratification can lead to a lot of spontaneous fun but its ramifications for business and economic development are negative. Americans employing Mexicans told me they will work all day so they can party late at night. They save too little so social infrastructures such as education, health, and housing suffer. Because of *mañana*, Mexican maintenance is an oxymoron. Everything from buses to plumbing is simply used until it stops working.

The Mexicans I met were fine people with a natural exuberance for life. Their art and music are beautiful. Perhaps it is expecting too much for them to give up some of today's pleasures in order to build a solid tomorrow.

The Arts

Mexican art explodes in rainbows of color. Wall murals, canvases, ceramics, textiles, and jewelry glow with the iridescence of the tropics: exquisite greens, garish oranges, bright ruby reds, deep indigos, haunting yellows, provocative pinks and purples.

Much Mexican art reflects social and political movements. The major feature of the post-Independence period was the rejection of Spain. At first artists, musicians, and authors with great emotion defined Mexico's feelings in terms of what Mexico was not. It took several generations and a revolution to finally shake out all the feelings of suppression and carve a culture unique to Mexico. Then painters were paid to cover public walls with murals depicting the suffering of the Indians under the Spanish and the creation of a new society.

Thus developed the distinctive Mexican style of mural painting, an art form related to the ancient markings in the caves of Altamira, the bas-relief wall carvings of the Aztecs and Mayans, and the garish graffiti of the Chicanos of East Los Angeles. I greatly enjoyed seeing the murals of Diego Rivera, José Clemente Orozco, and David Siqueros at the Palacio de Bellas Artes, the Museo Nacional de Artes Plásticas, and the Palacio Nacional. Some of Rivera's best murals are at the Ministry of Education. Painted in the 1920s, beautifully conceived, brilliantly colored, broadly panoramic, they burst with the intense vigor of Mexican village life.

Mexican mural art, which springs from the soil and those who work it, seems to balance and complement the rich pre-Columbian heritage of gold artifacts, stone carvings, and wooden statues displayed at the Museum of Anthropology in Xalapa, Veracruz, and the National Museum in Mexico City.

Music

Mexico holds the longest and largest tradition of European-style music in the New World. Soon after the Conquest

Spanish priests trained choirs of converted Aztecs to sing Gregorian chants in newly erected cathedrals. A choirmaster, Hernando Franco, produced the earliest American music now available on compact disks.

The polka, the foundation for much Mexican popular music, was introduced by the French during their occupation of Mexico in the 1860s.

The 1910 revolution endowed Mexican music with an authentic national flavor. Such serious composers as Manuel Ponce, Carlos Chávez, Julián Carrillo, and Silvestre Revueltas obtained international recognition.

Mexican folk music rivals Russia's and England's, offering songs and dances for every occasion. Its repertoire ranges from the performances of the deer dancers of the northwest desert to the soulful songs of the mariachis of Guadalajara. It explodes with emotion. In the United States a group of grown men singing so sensitively about love and romance would be laughed off the stage. Long ago the 1960s cultural revolution in the United States replaced such sentimental music with the rough, loud, sexual beats of rock. Instead of songs about roses and rain, young lovers, picking "our song," can choose "Do it in the dirt."

Language

Many people in the United States are familiar with the Spanish language. Los Angeles has more Spanish speakers than Madrid; only Mexico City has more. If current trends continue, in two generations half the population of the United States will speak Spanish.

While much is known about the linguistic nature of Spanish, less is known about its cultural significance. Like all languages it reflects and influences the values of its society.

Mexican Spanish is emotional and romantic. Laden with vowels, it lends itself to musical lyrics and the rhythm of poetry. It is as flowery as tropical foliage and as fiery as peppers. It is a ballet of nimble syllables which form subtle new meanings by swift prances around verb roots.

Spanish also reflects the fatalism of Mexican culture. Or is the culture fatalistic because of the language? By use of the reflexive *se* one avoids responsibility: "The vase broke on me." "The car had an accident on me."

Spanish can avoid commitment. *Mañana* becomes an unending stream of tomorrows which postpone business deadlines. The same verb, *esperar*, is used to mean *wait, hope* and *expect*, something to ponder when your Mexican counterpart is two hours late for a business appointment.

Spanish can be used protectively and evasively. This function is important when careless slights can puncture puffed-up pride; violence may seethe beneath the surface. The use of arcane honorifics can appear to lavish praise, make commitments, and offer explanations which are flowery but devoid of meaning. Political speeches are often garnished with grandiose slogans such as "revolution for the poor" which relate neither to revolution nor the poor.

Spanish can also smooth the way. Mexicans in abject poverty, with shreds for clothes, may use lace-cuff expressions derived from medieval Spanish courts, conversational embroidery such as "at your command," "your willing servant," and "grant me the favor." Polite diminutives soften commands. Third person forms of address serve as verbal glycerin: "What would the North American businessman suggest?"

Compared to people in the United States, Mexicans are more likely to discuss feelings than money. The ability to express oneself with *deep* feeling is admired. Mexicans can be so vehement that foreigners feel they are angry when they are not.

Spanish is strewn with wicked pitfalls for the neophyte speaker. In Oaxaca I ordered a hot dog by asking for a *perro caliente*, a "dog hot." This seemed to make sense because in Spanish the adjective usually follows the noun. Unfortunately in Spanish a *perro caliente* means "a bitch in heat." Guffaws. Smirks. Derogatory comments about demented gringos.

Literature

The magic cultures of the Aztecs and Mayans still live in Mexican literature. Writers compete with God in creating reality. With naïve pretension novelists alter the world in order to expand the sphere of possibilities. This genre is called magic realism. I was skeptical until I saw some of Mexico's true tropical enchantment: grotesquely-shaped trees blanketed by bright flowers with the exact shapes and colors of birds and butterflies; surreal brown dwarfs selling red-meated avocados the size of footballs, a two-foot tall midget, with a beautiful face, well-dressed and smiling, walking across a plaza on all fours like a crab.

Mexican writers are often involved in political debate and social causes. Some of their most powerful themes involve the conflict between Spanish and pre-Columbian Indian cultures and the violence of the Mexican Revolution. This literature, stressing social upheaval, is soberly realistic. Writers such as Mariano Azuela and José Rubén Romero Mexicanized Mexican literature, making it the most dynamic in Latin America.

Your Mexican business counterparts will be impressed if you take the trouble to learn about their literature. You could begin by reading some of the works of Carlos Fuentes and Octavio Paz. The essays and poems of Paz are broad in scope due to his knowledge of art, literature, culture, and society. Rosario Castellanos, Mexico's first modern feminist, wrote of the painful confrontation of Spanish and Mayan cultures. Her novel, *The Nine Guardians*, is a literary masterpiece. Armed conflicts in Chiapas are nothing new. They are chronicled by Eraclio Zepeda in short story collections such as *Benzulul* and *Pyramids of Glass*. Colonial period writers include Carlos de Sigüenza, a prose author; Sister Juana Inés de la Cruz, a lyrical poetess; and Juan Ruiz de Alarcón, a great dramatist.

Holidays and Festivals

Mexican holidays include New Year's Day; Constitution of 1917 Day (February 5); Flag Day (February 24); 1938 Oil Expropriation Day (March 18); the birthday of Benito Juárez (March 21); the Thursday, Friday, Saturday, and Sunday of Christian Holy Week; Labor Day (May 1); the 1862 Battle of Puebla versus the French Day (May 5); Mother's Day (May 10); 1810 Mexican Independence Day (September 16); and Mestizo Day (October 12).

The Days of the Dead (November 1 and 2) combine pre-Columbian and Catholic mysticism. Death is accepted with contempt. Skull-shaped pastries and candy coffins capture its images. Visits are made to family graves. Remaining holidays include the 1910 Day of Revolution (November 20); Day of Our Lady of Guadalupe (December 12) and Christmas.

If you employ Mexicans you will be surprised at the duration of holidays. Many Mexicans take *puente* (bridge) holidays which link regular holidays, thus avoiding work for weeks or even months. For the very devout there is a saint's day every day of the year.

Fiestas also provide opportunities for a break. Any family, ethnic, religious, civic, or patriotic occasion serves as an excuse. A fiesta provides a catharsis, a chance to escape rules and conventions, to vent emotions by shouting, singing, laughing, weeping, and firing bullets in the air; to break out of individual isolation and apathy, to create a spectacle with firecrackers, trumpets, and alcohol; to lose one's identity and morals while disguised in a bizarre costume. For Mexicans religious and patriotic fiestas are more than celebrations of past events; they reproduce them. Fiestas are the only entertainment for many Mexicans. So they and their villages spend extravagantly.

Cultural Change

Much has been written about the influence of Mexican culture on the United States. Cultural effects of the United

States on Mexico have been largely ignored. Yet these changes are far-reaching. They are driven by Mexico's contact with the United States through satellite television, increased trade (stimulated by NAFTA), and acquaintance with tourists from the United States. Along the northern border and in larger cities, Mexican culture is deeply influenced by such gringo values as individual independence, striving for success, and women's rights. Along both sides of the border a hybrid culture drawing on both Mexico and the United States, is rapidly emerging.

In many ways Mexico's growing middle class is using the United States as a model for its lifestyle. They prefer products from north of the border. Their children attend universities in the United States. Many middle class Mexican women now have good educations and hold responsible jobs, allowing them to obtain divorces when marriages are unhappy.

The language of Mexico is also changing. In the north words from the United States have immigrated to Mexico illegally. English words involving sports, entertainment, and technology now punctuate Spanish.

The agitation of cultural change will have both positive and negative effects. Mexico will experience more variety but anxiety will develop over new choices. The culture will become three-cornered: Spanish, pre-Columbian Indian, and North American Anglo.

2. *Family Life*

Family Structure

The Mexican concept of family involves an extended relationship including several generations, in-laws as remote as cousins of cousins, godparents, and friends in the local *barrio* (district). Long-time servants may also be drawn into the family structure. Like Mexican society, the family is paternalistic; like Mexican politics, it is authoritarian. Yet it provides abundant love and companionship. No one need ever be alone. (As an employer you will be expected to grant days off so families can celebrate the birthdays of members of the extended family.)

Despite severe pressures the family has been the bedrock of Mexican life. Without strong families Mexico's economic crises would have produced great social and political disruptions. Since Mexico has few government social programs, families are bound together by the glue of economic necessity: sheltering an unemployed cousin, minding a sister's child, caring for an elderly parent. In contrast close family cohesion in the United States has been undermined by increasing dependence on government programs such as day care, social security, welfare, and unemployment insurance.

The Spanish system of names reflects the importance of the family. Mexicans have dual last names, listing the father's family name first and the mother's family name second. When a women marries she keeps her father's surname but drops her mother's, replacing it with her husband's father's surname preceded by the article *de*. Maria Diego de Marquez has a name revealing her father's surname is Diego and her husband's father's surname is Marquez.

The Home

The Mexican home provides both emotional and physical sustenance. It is the one place where real emotions can be expressed. If you are invited to the home of your Mexican business counterpart consider it an honor.

Homemade meals, made from scratch, are desired over food which has been frozen, canned, dried or zapped in a microwave. Freshness is assured by daily visits to the market for meat and produce. Since many middle class wives work outside the home, a cook is usually hired. Depending on the affluence of the family there may be other servants: maids, watchmen, gardeners, and drivers. Some may work part-time. Middle class childen are likely to grow up without learning basic household skills. As adults they also will require servants.

The Mexican home is centered on meals and meals are centered on corn. Corn is to Mexico as rice is to Japan, a food laced with religious and patriotic significance. No food is more Mexican than the soft corn *tortilla*; the staff of life, the daily bread. *Tortillas* are made by soaking kernels of corn in limestone water and grinding them into *masa*, which is flattened and baked in disks. *Tortillas* are used as spoons, plates, and napkins as well as wrappers for *tacos, tostadas*, and *enchiladas*. These can contain a wide variety of delicious meats, vegetables, and sauces.

The Mexican diet varies with the location of the home. *Tacos, tamales*, and *enchiladas* originated on both sides of the Texas-Mexican border. The coasts produce fine seafood; the interior, excellent beef. Yucatán's cooking is part Cuban. Mexican seasoning ranges from pepper and *guacamole* sauces and lime juice to a *mole* sauce of spiced chocolate spread on poultry.

By custom every meal is a ceremony. Because Mexicans tend to stay up late at night, *desayuno*, breakfast, may be served later than in the United States. In the middle of the afternoon most Mexicans take a break from work. Many return home for the main meal of the day, *comida*, which is slow, leisurely and convivial. A *siesta* often follows. Maybe lost work time will be made up by returning to the job and working late. Maybe not.

If you plan to entertain Mexican business people, plan to serve cocktails between seven and eight. This allows plenty of time before *cena*, the light supper which is served between nine and ten. A snack, *bocatilla*, may be served anytime.

The Mexican family may enjoy entertainment by going together to parks, fiestas,and sporting events. But men, more than women, are more likely to go out alone. They may socialize with their male friends and watch sports on television in bars for men. Some of these drinking establishments are *pulquerías*, devoted to selling *pulque*, the thick, white, slightly sweet, fermented juice of the maguey plant.

Birth and Early Childhood

The birthrate in Mexico is decreasing, particularly among upper class and upwardly mobile middle class Mexicans. The government distributes free condoms. Abortions are illegal in Mexico but many poor women have them.

Most babies are baptized in the Catholic Church. A child's godfather and godmother accept the obligation to raise the child if its parents die. Often parents become godparents of each other's children creating a close bond.

Rural and working class mothers carry their infants in a *rebozo*, formed by wrapping cloth around the mother's midriff. There the baby, fed by breast, is safe and secure. It will occupy the *rebozo* until the next-born baby takes its place. Then it will be turned over to an older child for care. (Some female *gringas* have been known to wear *rebozos* with small dolls in them to forestall sexual harassment by Mexican men.)

Child raising has changed since the ancient Mayans disciplined children by rubbing pieces of hot peppers into their eyes. Today children are seldom punished. Caring for them seems to be a national pastime. Children are free to roam because the community accepts some responsibility for them. The process produces a curious, affectionate, alert, and secure child.

Adolescence

Since the 1992 transfer of basic education from the national government to the states, education through junior high school has been required. Yet, by adolescence many lower class children drop out of school.

At the age of fifteen many Mexican girls will be given special parties similar to those for debutantes in the United States. These are likely to involve a dance and a Catholic Mass. In many upper and middle class families, particularly in rural areas, the virginity of young women is still protected by a system of chaperones. In contrast young men have more sexual freedom.

In the cities dating patterns are more modern. Teenagers attend discos, movies, parties, and dances. Though teenage sex is slowly increasing, all but the lowest classes are very concerned about maintaining appearances. Young adults are more likely to live with their parents than alone. Single Mexican women are usually expected to live with their parents, relatives, or families approved by their parents. Propriety is important.

Marriage

Because of the separation of church and state only civil marriages are recognized in Mexico. An additional ceremony will usually take place in a church. The priest will require confession and instruction in matrimony before the wedding Mass and Communion are held. For the sake of family most wayward Mexican Catholics will go along with this procedure.

With marriage new sets of relationships develop. The bond created between both families is tighter than in the United

States. Both fathers of a married couple are called *consuegro*, both mothers, *consuegra*. American English does not deem this relationship sufficiently important to warrant titles.

In a traditional Mexican marriage the husband is considerably older than the wife. The wife stays home with the children while the husband goes to work. Her role as mother is glorified because Mexican men adore their own mothers. However, mothers-in-law are different. There are many Mexican mother-in-law jokes. The mother-in-law in the lyrics of the famous song, "El Rancho Grande," is buried face down "so she will dig herself deeper if she tries to get out!"

The Male Sexual Dilemma

Mexican men suffer from a severe sexual vulnerability which has historical antecedents. During the Spanish conquest many Indian women were raped by the invaders; others willingly betrayed their men. Most Mexicans are *mestizos*, progeny of the rape of one culture by another. A famous Mexican expletive is *hijo de la chingada*, "son of a raped woman."

In relations with women, Mexican men must deal with confused feelings of guilt, shame, and betrayal. Should they identify with the Spaniard's domination of women or the humiliation of the Indian? In either case affection and faithfulness are signs of weakness. So the Mexican male wears macho armor to shield his fragile libido. The swagger of adultery fronts as a façade for his bewildered sexual emotions.

Most Mexican men place their mothers on pedestals, the proper place for givers of life as pure as the Virgin of Guadalupe. Every man wants a wife like his mother. When he finds her he pushes her down and humiliates her because she fulfills the pure-mother role sufficiently to be rejected as a sexual partner but insufficiently to be adored. Besides, loyalty and commitment to a wife could make a husband vulnerable to betrayal and pain. This justifies male promiscuity or the keeping of a mistress in a separate "little house."

Not every marriage takes this pattern. But most wives who experience it respond by giving the love refused by their husbands to their sons. Sons become surrogate fathers. Mexican mothers often call their small sons *papito*, "little father." They counter the neglect of their husbands by building a power base from their children. Their sons will grow up to idolize their mothers and deprecate their wives, continuing the cycle.

Work

The frontier of the United States was a gritty, grimy place where farmers and miners sweated to carve a living from the earth. In comparison Spain's eight hundred year campaign to expel the Moors was led by warriors, priests, and poets who felt the dirt of common labor would soil the nobility of their mission. When they conquered Mexico they made the Indians do all the hard manual work.

The conditioning of different national histories has resulted in great contrasts in attitudes towards menial labor. Many middle class Mexicans employ house servants while most middle class people in the United States do their own housework. Young middle class Mexicans eschew part-time jobs such as waiting on tables and janitorial work. This contrasts with the attitude in the United States where even children of affluent parents might do menial work to develop independence and separate identities.

Many people in the United States live to work, pursuing careers which lend purpose to their lives. Most Mexicans work to live. Some of their *gringo* employers told me "they will work hard all day so they can party hard all night."

Old Age and Death

In Mexican families the old usually take care of the very young. The young then take care of the old when they can no longer function.

When a family member dies a wake is held. By law disposal of the body must take place within twenty-four hours.

Mexicans approach death directly: they mock it. On the Days of the Dead in November they defiantly consume skull-shaped candies and take food to graveyards. For them death is conquered by the continuity of life. The past and present merge because all life is life after death.

What Kind of Person?

What kind of person does the Mexican family system produce? The answers are important for your understanding of your Mexican business counterpart.

Your Mexican will have a strong sense of personal honor and dignity. He or she will display a warm sentimentality and a deep sensitivity to arts such as music and dance. In contrast to the emotional inhibitions of the Anglo heritage, your Mexican will release a rich array of spontaneous feelings. In periods of solitude or meditation he or she will store up immense inner strengths to face the harsh vicissitudes of life.

Yet this same person may be selfish and pompous, delighting in conspicuous consumption such as ostentatious weddings and a superfluous entourage of retainers. Though titles were abolished by the 1910 Revolution, feelings of hubris are fed with such honorifics as *licenciado* for college graduates and *maestro* for teachers.

The dark side gets darker. The male sexual dilemma often produces domestic violence, illegitimate children, absent fathers, and lonely mothers who must be mainstays. Families produce the people who contribute to Mexico's chaotic negligence: uncollected garbage, smog-permeated air, polluted water, inoperable plumbing, and ignored traffic rules. There is little social consciousness, no volunteer tradition, and few private efforts at community improvements such as orphanages. Most of these are established and operated by charitable foreigners.

3. Politics and Law

Political Origins: Indian and Spanish

Mexican politics is deeply rooted in the absolutism of Spanish Catholicism and the theocracy of the Aztecs. Military conquest and coerced religious conversion were expediently intertwined: the sword and the crucifix, blood, death, suffering, people on their knees.

Montezuma considered the arrival of Cortés, a white-bearded man bearing crosses, to be a fulfillment of ancient Aztec prophecy which foretold the return of Quetzalcoatl, a legendary white-bearded god who may have been a Viking, ship-wrecked sailor, or fanatical Christian missionary.

For 250 years after the Spanish conquest, the Inquisition officiated in Mexico burning some victims and scorching the lives of others. Both of the New Left priests who led Mexico's struggle for independence were condemned by the Inquisition in order to justify their executions by political authorities.

Common Mexicans, pinioned by political and religious oppression, cried out for revolution. It soon surged up in great turbulent billows inundating Mexico with blood.

Three Revolutions

The onslaught came in three waves. The first revolution won independence from Spain. The second established partial and temporary political and economic reform. The third, the one Mexicans call *the* Mexican revolution, pitted the poor and dispossessed against the rich oligarchy of General Porfirio Díaz.

In Mexico's first revolution a landed class of feudal leaders gave lip service to democracy in order to get peasant support for a revolution which freed their estates from Spanish control. Thus began the Mexican tradition of using the rhetoric of democracy as a façade for oligarchic purposes. Two priests became martyrs for independence. Both died with much *machismo*. Father Hidalgo, captured, defrocked, and sentenced, was executed after thanking his killers for their hospitality, giving them candy, and praying for them. Father José Morelos was captured and shot just before Christmas 1815, leaving a thank-you note to his guards scrawled on the wall of his cell in his own blood. Others continued the fight. In 1821 Mexico finally achieved independence from Spain under Agustin de Iturbide, a Spanish military officer who changed his allegiance from Spain to the rebels. Iturbide promptly named himself emperor of Mexico. The nation's social and political structure barely changed. His generals received huge grants of land. Slavery was abolished but not poverty. Poor landless Indians still worked the fields.

The failure of Mexico's first revolution led to a second. Benito Juárez, a Zapotec Indian, like an Aztec priest, grabbed the heart of the matter by leading a violent revolt against economic privilege, the caste system, and clericalism. When France took advantage of the U.S. Civil War by invading Mexico and setting up Maximilian as emperor, Juárez escaped to the deserts of northern Mexico and waged guerrilla war. In 1867 France, embroiled in Europe, withdrew its forces, leaving Maximilian stranded. Juárez executed him on the Hill of Bells near Querétaro.

For a while Mexico's second revolution succeeded in placing all citizens under the same law by abolishing special courts for the clergy and military. Juárez changed Mexico from a colonial clone consisting of ruling Spanish purebloods and subservient *mestizos* and Indians to a nation imbued with a revolutionary spirit of Mexicanism. But change was not easy. In destroying the temporal power of Catholicism the revolution confiscated the Church's huge land holdings, burned cathedrals, and slaughtered priests. Faithful old women, unable to accept the new order, soaked their handkerchiefs in the blood of slain priests and used them to bless themselves.

With the victory of Juárez, Mexicans reconquered their own nation. Though the spirit of reform was strong, its body was weak. Failure to implement the goals of reform led to the long dictatorship of Porfirio Díaz.

Mexico's third revolution was directed against Díaz. He ruled Mexico in person or by proxy from 1877 to 1911. His policies emphasized rapid economic progress by and for Mexico's elite. Manufacturing, agriculture, and transportation, though greatly expanded, became concentrated in the hands of rich Mexicans and foreigners. Progress came on the backs of the poor. Díaz used violence to stop strikes by growing numbers of disgruntled industrial workers. Seething rural resentment contributed to the rise of revolutionary leaders such as Pancho Villa and Emiliano Zapata. Even middle class Mexicans could not accept ownership of millions of acres of Mexican land, mineral resources, banks, railways, and utilities by foreigners, particularly Americans. At times even Díaz lamented that Mexico was so close to the United States and so far from God.

As 1910 approached Villa and Zapata fanned the fires of revolution. Within a decade over a million Mexicans were killed, one out of every fifteen. Zapata shot the owners of large haciendas, giving the land to poor peons. Villa was an erratic romantic who loved looting and burning. After the United States shifted support to Villa's rival, Carranza, Villa invaded New Mexico on a murderous rampage, then retreated into Mexico. A penetration of Mexico by General "Black Jack" Pershing failed to capture Pancho, who knew how to dance with his enemies. In time both Zapata and Villa were assassinated by political rivals.

Many Mexicans looked at the limited results of these revolutions and felt used and betrayed. When all was said and done more was said than done. "Viva la Revolución" became a byword in passionate political speeches but few wished to repeat the experience. There had been too much terror for too little change. Most Mexicans settled down to accept a long period of one-party rule. Much of the bloodshed stopped but Mexican politics devolved into a dreary succession of dictators taking power through intimidation, fraud, rebellion, coups, and assassinations. The common Mexican, frustrated and demoralized, withdrew into himself, contemplating his condition in a Pazian labyrinth of solitude. A cabby in Mexico City summarized the situation in response to my standard question about the likelihood of another Mexican revolution: "No señor, we have had enough revolutions to know they do little good."

Constitution and Government

Mexico's most important political institutions date from the 1910 Revolution and its aftermath. The 1917 Constitution strengthened the power of the state particularly the executive branch. Its authors mistakenly assumed the state would use its new powers to carry out the ideals of the revolution. Though there were political, agrarian, and labor reforms, the structure of the new constitution was used to keep a dominant party in power.

The president, elected by a direct vote, is limited to a single six-year term, a restriction of power with little meaning because each outgoing president has picked his successor. There is no vice president. If the president dies or is disabled during the first two years of a term, new elections are held. After the first two years Congress selects a replacement president to complete the term. The cabinet consists of leaders of twenty-one departments.

The legislature, also elected by popular vote, consists of a senate comprised of two members per state and federal district elected for six-year terms and a lower house consisting of chamber deputies elected for three-year terms.

The judicial branch is headed by twenty-one supreme court judges appointed for life by the president with approval of the senate. No supreme court judge has ever opposed a major presidential policy. The court has used its power to suspend laws only when such action favors presidential policies.

Though thirty-one provinces and a federal district elect their own governors, judges, and legislatures, their power is weak. Provincial officials may be removed by a vote of the national senate.

The Constitution provides for a military force. But Mexico needs only a small one. It could never be large enough to oppose the U.S. Army and almost any size is big enough to handle its weak southern neighbors. There is no need to prepare for invasion from outside the continent because such an event would surely trigger U.S. intervention. The Mexican army need only be large enough to suppress internal dissent such as the recent uprisings in Chiapas.

Politics

Because of the dominant role of culture no constitution can ensure individual rights and democratic processes. As an example the incredible power and supreme respect accorded the Mexican president is derived, not from a constitution, but from deeply-rooted cultural traditions: the awesome powers of Aztec emperors, the contumely of Mayan priests, and the infallibility of Roman popes. Fortunately part of the president's power is ceremonial façade designed to satisfy the abnormal need of Mexicans for a supreme unifying national power.

Like the culture, one-party rule undermines the Constitution. Since 1934 all presidents have been members of the dominant Institutional Revolutionary Party (PRI). The resources of the state—money, trucks, labor, and loudspeakers—have been freely employed to win elections and keep the PRI in power. The common Mexican going to vote may find that the polling place is not where it should be. It may open late. Officials, ballots, and ink may be missing. The count is often strangely delayed.

Many Mexicans in order to survive simply accept the power of the ruling class. The up-and-coming ward heeler I met in Oaxaca was busy providing Carta Blanca beer for barrio parties and pressing the flesh of potential voters. Yet he had probably made an accommodation with *el Jefe*, the local boss. The peasant confronting injustice has learned to seek, not legal rights but the personal largess of a paternalistic power broker. There are no government entitlements, just favors.

One who has a problem with the law becomes a problem for the legal system, which is often arbitrary and corrupt, run by men rather than public mandate. There is no bill of rights and no independent judiciary. Mexico follows the Napoleonic Code, which assumes one is guilty until proven innocent. There are documented cases of police resorting to intimidation, extortion, and torture to obtain confessions. Many Mexican lawyers are no better. Like some of their *gringo* counterparts they practice law in the same way prostitutes practice love.

Parties

The PRI has dominated Mexican politics for over sixty years by controlling the political center of such diverse groups as farmers, business, labor, and media. It preempts new causes, issues, and positions before they produce substantial opposition. Because it tries to please all groups the PRI's policies often seem contradictory. It supports privatization while whooping revolutionary slogans, rigs elections while cracking down on corruption, and lowers corn tariffs while parroting the plight of poor Indian corn farmers.

In some ways the power of the PRI is weakening. The loss of government-owned industries to privatization leaves fewer jobs and benefits to parcel out in return for political support. Mexico's membership in the North American Free

Trade Agreement makes the use of anti-Americanism less effective as a means to rile up domestic support. The television and the press are becoming more independent. During the 1994 election campaign pro-government television networks showed speeches of non-PRI presidential candidates for the first time.

To Mexico's credit it does have opposition parties. The National Action Party (PAN) is strongest along the U.S. border and Yucatán. In 1989 it won the governorship of Baja. Its conservative, business-oriented platform has been undermined somewhat by the PRI's moves toward privatization and NAFTA.

The Party of Democratic Revolution (PRD) is the major force on the left. Some members formerly belonged to the disbanded Mexican socialist party. The PRD, the party of small farmers and industrial workers, is concerned with election fraud, agrarian causes, and labor reform. Like most leftist parties it realizes it must deal with the government. The alternative would be a military regime. In a few areas, such as Chiapas, the violence of confrontations between leftist rebels and the army probably precludes meaningful negotiation.

Foreign Policy

Mexico's foreign policy is driven by its geographical propinquity to the United States. Mexico is not free to enter foreign alliances inimical to U.S. interests. It must keep on good terms with the United States to avoid economic and political punishment. Its problem is how to maintain a degree of independence while dependent on the U.S. for tourism, export markets, private investment, bank loans and the earnings of millions of Mexican workers in the United States.

Mexico's political leadership, though conservative at home, has often supported revolutions in nations such as Cuba and Nicaragua. It thus deflects U.S. attention from Mexico and validates its revolutionary ideals to its own people.

For people in the United States the war with Mexico is almost lost in memory. Not so for Mexicans. They remember not only the war, which resulted in loss of almost two-thirds of Mexico to the United States, but invasions by U.S. generals Scott and Pershing. Hatred of the United States is still a cornerstone of Mexican nationalism. Even crises of completely domestic origin are blamed on the colossus of the north. Sometimes Mexican feelings of persecution become paranoiac. Some Mexicans think the U.S. wants to stop Mexican immigration as a ploy to obtain lower oil prices. Others think a drought in Yucatán took place because the U.S. seeded the rain out of the clouds before they could get to Mexico. It is easy to conjure up conspiracies between the U.S. Immigration Service, weather agencies, and big oil companies.

Mexican presidents seem to need conservative U.S. presidents as foils. President López Portillo, speaking of President Carter, once said that having a U.S. president positioned to his left threatened his political survival.

Mexico's relations with the United States are impeded by ignorance of our political system. Mexican leaders, used to a system in which power emanates from a powerful president, have difficulty understanding the U.S. system of checks and balances. To some Mexican officials our three branches of government look like three governments. They fail to realize the U.S.Constitution was not designed to impose orderly and efficient government but to guarantee individual freedoms.

Recent Politics

The PRI's opening from the center seems to be working for it. In recent years its dependence on fraud to win elections has diminished. In the 1988 elections the left-wing National Democratic Front won the large urban centers. But the PRI controlled the tabulation and won the presidency by fraudulent returns from rural areas under its control. "The computers melted down!"

Six years later in August 1994 the PRI's presidential candidate, Ernesto Zedillo Ponce de León, a career technocrat with a doctorate in economics, won an impressive victory in a reasonably fair election. He promised to continue PRI policies of encouraging foreign investment, continuing privatization of industry, and improving infrastructure. Zedillo also promised he would end the practice of outgoing presidents naming the PRI's next presidential candidate.

There are real political reforms taking place in Mexico. Some members of the PRI Old Guard seeing their power wane may be responding with violence. Several reformist politicians have been assassinated, including the PRI's initial presidential candidate in the 1994 election, Luis Donaldo Colosio. Political savagery is as Mexican as *tortillas*. It will be hard to change.

Political Prospects

How can Mexico develop into a mature democracy? In the early twentieth century the answer was to establish a constitution. Mexico did so, but its effectiveness was impeded by economic and cultural traditions. In time Mexicans came to the realization that political systems are based on culture and cultures change slowly. If Mexican democracy is to take root it must seek nutrients from the soil of Mexico's unique culture. It must come to terms with its authoritarian tradition without reverting to the dungeons of the Inquisition. In short it must find its own way to modernity.

The true test of a democracy occurs when a party in power, voted out of power, leaves peacefully. In time the PRI will lose an election. Will it then break the Mexican tradition of transfer of power between parties only through coups, assassinations, and revolutions? We shall see.

Perhaps economics will lead the way. The emerging nations of Asia offer a hopeful pattern. There improved economies created middle classes which gained considerable power by following an old adage: power follows money. To understand the dynamics of this process and its implications for business enterprises we need to take a look at the development and operation of the Mexican economy, our next topic.

PART TWO

Economy and Business

With the passage and implementation of the North American Free Trade Agreement (NAFTA), Mexico's economy and businesses have assumed new importance. Events in Mexico are moving with incredible speed. New opportunities and risks abound.

To operate successfully in Mexico you will need to understand how its economy developed and functions, its problems, strengths, and weaknesses. In addition to addressing these topics, this section will help you with some of the practical aspects of doing business in Mexico. These include how to get help, deal with the Mexican business system, and conduct business bargaining. These activities are strongly influenced by the cultural and social topics just covered. Mexican business people, like business people everywhere, are people first.

This book is designed to be a general guide and does not offer legal or accounting advice. Every business situation is different. Rules and regulations are constantly changing. For the most recent detailed information, contact the organizations listed in chapters nine and thirteen.

4. *A Brief Economic History*

Pre-Columbian Period

Possibly the major difference between the economic development of Mexico and the United States involves the fate of the Indians. In the United States warlike nomadic Indian tribes were exterminated or confined to reservations. The Indian hunting economy, including the buffalo, had to be destroyed so settlers could build a new farming economy. In Mexico most Indians were already farmers. After the Conquest they were integrated into the Spanish economic system. Mexico was built on well-developed Indian economic foundations.

We should not romanticize the life of pre-Hispanic Indians. In the shadows of the great pyramids, the Indian workers who built them ate boiled beans and corn *tortillas*, lived in pest-filled huts, and suffered diseases and exploitation.

But they built a viable economy. By 3500 B.C. corn cultivation replaced hunting and gathering. Corn had deep religious significance. All life, including human, seemed derived from it. Beans, planted in the same holes, climbed the stalks. Squash and pumpkins edged the corn fields. These were supplemented by sweet potatoes, chili peppers, cassava, papayas, avocados, peanuts, guava, chocolate, chayote (a green vegetable) and the meat of domesticated turkeys. As always the wealthy ate better.

Gold and silver metallurgy began in Mexico about A.D. 1000. Beautiful objects crafted in these metals were exported far distances. Other articles for trade included obsidian knives, emeralds, feather weavings, chocolate, vanilla, bat-wings, fur, rubber, quinine, tobacco, and a variety of narcotics. So old is the drug trade! Mexico's Aztec and Mayan Indians used an area in what is now modern Belize as an entrepôt for indirect trade with the Incas of South America.

Colonial Period

The Spanish Conquistadors simply wanted to milk Mexico of its treasures so they could go home rich. According to a contemporary chronicler, Bernard Díaz, Montezuma made the mistake of telling Cortés "my house is your house." Cortes then took all the Aztec's possessions: house, treasure, country. All the precious gold art treasures created by Montezuma's incredibly skilled artisans were melted down by the Spanish and sent to Spain in the form of bars to finance wars and intrigues in Europe. Within a half century of the Conquest the Spanish had located all the Aztec mines. Gold, silver, and copper gushed from the soil, enriching the new aristocrats. To this day Mexican silverwork is world famous.

Mexico's greatest wealth was found, not in gold, but in the labor of millions of Indians who were forced to work for little if any wages. They did the farming, ranching, mining, dye production (red cochineal and blue indigo), and sugar refining which made Mexico's rulers prosperous. Cheap Indian labor was assured through the *encomienda* system in which the Spanish king delegated the right to collect Indian tribute and labor to the Conquistadors and their progeny. Thus a remnant of European feudalism, the right of a lord over his serfs, was transferred to the New World. By the time the *encomienda* system was softened it had created a division of society into an upper class of large landowners and an under class of agricultural debt peons which was to have a profound effect on Mexico's economy and politics.

Spain's strangle hold on Mexican trade was as tight as its suffocating grip on the Indians. The mother country outlawed production of wine or olive oil in Mexico in order to create a captive market for its own products. (Without local wine the Mexicans brewed beer.) In order to maintain its own monopoly the Spanish crown banned direct Mexican trade with any other country. All Mexican trade had to move through Spanish ports. Taxes were imaginative, ubiquitous, fissiparous, and unfair. Until the late eighteenth century there was little concern for improving the infrastructure. Then the Mexican viceroy, Count Revilla Gigeda II, built roads and street lights, constructed water systems and schools, and established public health facilities.

For most of the colonial period the management of Mexico's economy by selfish, petty, myopic Spanish functionaries was so corrupt and arbitrary that it impeded the development of commerce and industry by stifling incentives and free markets. Today Mexico still wrestles with the problems of throwing off the debilitating effects of its Spanish economic heritage.

Revolutionary Agronomics

Mexico's three revolutions were largely concerned with land reform. In colonial times the Catholic Church had a lock on the economy. It owned huge tracts of agricultural land. It controlled the opinions of farm labor through its monopoly of education. The police and army were sympathetic to the few privileged which owned the large *haciendas*.

It was not until *la Reforma* under Benito Juárez that Church and State were separated. Still later, after the 1910 Revolution, *haciendas* were broken up and replaced by *ejidos*, where groups or individuals exercised rights to farm government land. Though *ejidos* provide land for most Mexican farmers, they have produced poorly due to lack of education of farmers in the basics of agriculture and the intense competition of agri-businesses using large-scale credit, modern machinery, and the scientific application of seeds, water, and fertilizer. Much of this large-scale agriculture is owned by politicians and generals who benefited from Mexico's revolutions more than the peons who died for them. No matter the system the peasant remained mired in poverty.

The response to the Mexican government's inability to fulfill agrarian revolutionary reforms was predictable. On New Year's Day, 1994, more than a hundred people were killed in a peasant revolt in Chiapas led by Sub-comandante Marcos. Other less violent incidents erupted in the states of Tabasco, Oaxaca, Mexico, Yucatán, Veracruz, Guerrero, Michocan, and Puebla. Members of the Chiapas Mayan army called themselves Zapatistas after the half-breed revolutionary whose battle cry was "land and liberty!" These Indians had fought for Mexico in wars against Spain, France, and the United States. Still landless, they felt betrayed. This time they decided to be cannon fodder for themselves. They took no heed of Vice President Albert Gore's declaration on the eve of the revolt: "Mexico is now stable." Until Mexico, a land dependent upon the fruits of its soil, finds a way to extend benefits more widely, its harvests are likely to be measured in rebellions rather than bushels. As your com-pany's Mexican expert you will be expected to evaluate such political risks.

War of 1848

The War of 1848, which Mexicans call "the War of the Yankee Invasion," resulted in the loss of almost two-thirds of Mexico to the United States. Mexicans who remained in this large area from Kansas to California contributed to the economy of the United States, not Mexico's. Recently discovered gold in California financed an industrial revolution in the United States, not Mexico. The cotton fields of Texas fed the spinning mills of New England, not Monterrey.

The people of Mexico would never forget.

The Díaz Period

President Porifirio Díaz tried to modernize Mexico through foreign investment and trade. He developed industry and private enterprise, built railroads and reduced the national debt. Mexico became the major recipient of U.S. foreign investment and the world's second largest oil exporter.

Unfortunately much of this economic progress came on the backs of the poor. Díaz restored class privileges which had been abolished by Juárez. Most of Mexico's major industries were now owned by foreigners. Little trickled down. Common Mexicans suffered declining living standards. They hungered for food, work, and land.

The Revolution of 1910 was fought for economic reasons. It began with strikes and peasant revolts directed at the Díaz dictatorship. The fight for redistribution of feudal estates and labor rights was led in the north by Emiliano Zapata and in the south by Francisco Villa. Mexico's Revolution, more emotional than ideological, exploded in a magical fiesta of bullets, a jubilant release of energy. It was a time for trumpets, rockets, and gunfire, a chance to free long-leashed feelings and open the veins. It basted Mexico with blood.

The Role of Oil

Oil has always been a combustible topic in Mexico. Energy underlies all economic development and oil is a major source of energy. Mexico is self-sufficient in oil and has huge reserves. This gift of nature has produced an abundance of riches and troubles.

Mexican oil was discovered near Tampico in 1901 by an American, Edward Doheny. Big multi-national oil companies soon set up operations. There was an oil boom during World War I but it ended with the war. Demand and prices plummeted during the Great Depression.

In 1938, pinched by the Great Depression, Mexico expropriated its oil industry. The United States did not oppose this takeover because World War II was developing and the United States was concerned about a possible alliance between Mexico and Nazi Germany. Mexican oil, now nationalized came under the control of Pemex, a state petroleum company. It could never decide whether to be a profit-making company or a money-losing social service. Like most Mexican institutions it was stunted by corruption, nepotism, and union bossism. The 1940-1982 economic expansion triggered by World War II masked many of these problems.

The 1970s was the decade of oil. Shifting demand, supply and prices rocked the world as much as a world war. World dependence on crude oil shifted to the Middle East at a time of war and Arab oil embargo. World prices for crude oil rocketed from two dollars to thirty-two dollars per barrel. At this time of acute shortages, of gas lines and cold buildings, huge new reserves were discovered in Mexico.

For the Mexican government this oil might as well have been alcohol. The bureaucracy intoxicated by the windfall spent lavishly and postponed difficult decisions. President Portillo said his biggest problem was "administering the abundance." Mexico's economic roller coaster ride began with an illusive boom. Both public and private parties leveraged oil income by borrowing heavily abroad.

Unfortunately for Mexico the economic dominoes started falling. The impact of high oil prices by producing inflation and high interest rates knocked down the world economy. One by one the pieces fell in a spreading recession. With reduced demand Mexico's oil prices and its economy tumbled. World economic events forced Mexico into an austerity it had been unable to impose on itself. Now fell the dominoes of atonement: devaluation of the peso, rigid exchange controls, freezing of dollar deposits, and coerced conversion of dollars in Mexico into less valuable pesos. In 1981, just before the last click, the Mexican government announced it could not pay its debts. Then silence.

But not from the large U.S. banks which had lent and lost money. Through loud lamentations and vociferous whining they finagled loan guarantees from both the U.S. and Mexican governments. In return these banks had to forgive part of Mexico's debt. In order to obtain U.S. dollars to repay debt, Mexico had to reduce imports and increase exports, thus going back on the import substitution policy which had caused many of the problems in the first place.

After a second oil bubble burst in 1986 the Mexican government, as debased as its currency, experienced an epiphany, a sudden manifestation of the essence of something: the Mexican economy was subject to world forces outside its control. Armed with this insight the government stopped prostrating itself before the gods of fate and rose to the challenge of producing drastic reforms.

Yet its oil is still the pride of Mexico. In the summer of]994 I had the pleasure of lunch with Dr. Elena Cardero, who negotiated the energy portion of NAFTA for Mexico. It was no accident that Mexico deployed its most personable and skilled negotiator on behalf of its most highly prized asset, oil. It is no surprise that under NAFTA Mexican oil remains nationalized.

Economic Reforms

The Mexican government, heir of the class revolution of 1910, did not freely shift the economy from socialism to capitalism. This change, forced by domestic as well as international circumstances was exemplified by an August 1982 wire services photo of a Mexican woman weeping inside a Tijuana bank after learning the money she had saved from fourteen years of picking tomatoes had lost seventy-five per cent of its value because the Mexican government devalued the peso.

Mexico's malady had been festering for a long time. Until the mid-1980s the economy was excessively regulated, artificially protected, and grossly inefficient. It was characterized by state monopolies, nationalized industries, high tariffs, and tight restrictions on foreign investment. These policies, inherited from Spanish colonialism, produced the worst of all possible worlds: roaring inflation tied to collapsing prices for Mexico's export commodities, shortages of investment capital needed to replace outmoded plant and machinery, and an addiction to foreign loans at a time of decreasing foreign trade. Both Mexican laborers and investors took one look at the situation and fled the country. The government was left with only two choices: economic reform or political revolution. For the party in power decisions could no longer be postponed. There might be no more *mañanas*.

Finally the government reacted. It realized it needed an economic policy more sensible than simply devaluing the peso and rescheduling debt. Under President Miguel de la Madrid (1982-88) and his successor, Carlos Salinas de Gortari, Mexico knocked down many restrictive dikes of regulation and released a deluge of reforms: dropping of trade restrictions, stopping of subsidies (even for corn *tortillas*), an anti-inflation pact with business and labor, privatization of many state industries, relaxation of foreign investment restrictions, and improved protection of intellectual property. The income from sales of state industries to private parties was used to reduce the national debt. As part of its epiphany Mexico realized it could not go it alone. In 1986 it joined the General Agreement on Tariffs and Trade (GATT): in 1994 it joined the North American Free Trade Association (NAFTA). This was a sharp departure from its old policy of attacking "Yankee imperialism."

The result was a booming economy based largely on private initiative, increased competition, return of capital from abroad, lower inflation, increased gross domestic product, and expanded consumer purchasing power. Market pricing made the economy more efficient. Increased investment improved productivity. Private rather than public ownership stimulated incentive. Under President Salinas (1988-94) public debt dropped from seventy-five per cent to thirty-three per cent of GDP. Annual inflation slowed from fifty-two per cent to an astounding five per cent.

In attempting to slow an economy which was overheating with success, the government bit the brakes too hard. By mid-1994, Mexico was mired in another recession. Though much had been accomplished much still needed to be done. Mexico's new economic discipline had improved the general economy but many Mexicans had been left behind. Both government services and wages for working people had been cut.

NAFTA

Octavio Paz, Mexico's greatest poet and essayist, favored NAFTA because it represented a chance for Mexico to drop the baggage of medieval Spain and become a modern nation with faith in change such as the United States.

President Salinas staked his political career on passage of NAFTA. Effective on January 1, 1994, it came on the heels of other international agreements creating the largest free trade area in the world. It deserves more attention and will receive it in some of the following chapters.

5. A Look at Mexico's Economy

Change?

The government is trying to modernize Mexico's economy by following a proven pattern: privatization, increased foreign investment, deregulation, and participation in international economic organizations. These policies have already produced substantial results. Yet a regnant question remains: will the effectiveness of Mexico's new economic strategy be undermined by a cultural lag inherent in an archaic social system which never accepted the Dogma of Progress of the Enlightenment? Only time will tell.

Mexico is no United States. Its economy needs just about everything. For four hundred years Mexico has accepted the poverty of half its population. Population growth is too fast due to Catholic prohibitions on birth control. One in four Mexicans is under the age of fifteen. Education is inadequate. Per capita income is about $3,400 per year resulting in individual purchasing power about one-sixth that of people in the United States. Hourly compensation for typical workers, including all fringe benefits, is only about $2.50 per hour.

Recent economic reforms act like pancake make-up, making Mexico more presentable in the international economic community. But they vainly conceal the flaws of an archaic social and political system. Stigma of corruption erupt. Violent rebellions inflame Chiapas, chilling the Mexican stock market. The bureaucracy opens only for a privileged few, providing loopholes, even black holes. No analysis of Mexico's economy can be complete without addressing its central problem: the conflict between economic modernization and the cultural residue of a medieval past.

Infrastructure

Mexico's infrastructure, from communication to transportation, is rudimentary but improving. In response to a need for better communication the Mexican government privatized the state-owned Telefonos de Mexico by selling part of it to a foreign group including Southwestern Bell. It also opened up a wide range of communication manufacturing and services to private enterprise. Though the results are encouraging, success has been overrated. Telmex should not have such heavy weighting on the Mexican stock index because it derives about half of its income from phone calls (in dollars) from the United States to Mexico. This provides it with more protection against peso devaluations than most Mexican companies.

Mexico's booming road construction is partly propelled by the profit motive of entrepreneurs building toll roads. Until 1989, trucking was controlled by a few large companies which kept rates high. Now there are many trucking operators; service has improved; prices have declined. But much of Mexico's transportation equipment is antiquated. Maintenance is poor; training, inadequate. Buses I took from Belize through Yucatán, and up the east coast had been discarded by companies in the United States because they no longer passed safety tests. Two drivers each worked twelve-hour shifts. The off-duty driver slept on a mattress in the luggage compartment. Such exhaustion contributed to an accident in Yucatán while I was there. The driver tangled his bus in some power lines. It became a toaster. His passengers became breakfast pop-ups. No one survived.

Other Mexican transportation systems have critical needs. Airports need expansion. Ports need modernization. Though about eighty per cent of Mexico's freight moves by rail, the National Railway needs new rolling stock. There are many bottlenecks.

Much of Mexico has no electric power. But the construction of power plants is accelerating. In 1994 President Zedillo announced a twelve-year program to double electric power capacity.

Half of all Mexicans have no flush toilets. One in three has no indoor potable water. Public toilets, such as those in government buildings, rail and bus stations, are consistently out of order.

The federal government is trying to empower Mexican states and municipalities to meet local infrastructure needs. The transition will not be easy. Mexico's tradition of a powerful paternalistic central government precludes, or at least impedes, independent initiative by local governments.

One of the most common complaints I heard from U.S. business people in Mexico concerned the cost of building communications, power, transportation, and water systems to service new plants. Some felt such costs wiped out the savings achieved by employing cheap Mexican labor.

Agriculture

Most Mexican agriculture is located around Mexico City and the valleys to the south. Corn is the staple crop. Cash crops include pineapple, bananas, coffee, cocoa, sugar cane, cotton, wheat, and a variety of fruits and vegetables.

The image of Mexico as a tropical cornucopia for food production is false. Mexico, a net importer of food, is unable to feed its burgeoning population. Agriculture has steadily declined as a percentage of gross domestic product. Except for winter fruits and vegetables, NAFTA is not producing a huge influx of Mexican agriculture products into the United States.

Many factors limit the success of Mexican agriculture. Much of the nation is too high and too dry for crops. In the Yucatán rain soaks too quickly through the ground. Only about ten per cent of Mexico's land is ideal for farming. Too much of Mexico's agricultural production consists of commodities such as sugar, wheat, coffee, and cotton, which are subject to world-wide price fluctuations.

Though the government has instituted considerable agricultural land reform, Mexican farmers have been slow to take advantage of it. In contrast, during the three years I lived in Taiwan I observed a land reform which produced a class of alert, price-conscious small farmers which quickly changed crops from price-vulnerable commodities such as sugar cane and bananas to high value-added products such as farmed shrimp, canned mushrooms, Mandarin oranges, and gourmet tea. Though Mexico has had no similar agricultural revolution, there are scattered instances of successful responses to government initiatives. Federal investments in water projects in northwestern Mexico have made Sinaloa and Sonora major producers of fruits and vegetables for the U.S. winter market. With urbanization processed breakfast cereals and baby foods are becoming popular. Food processing is emerging as a growth industry.

The opportunities for agricultural corporations are growing. The agrarian law of February 1992 produced sweeping changes. Land is no longer expropriated for distribution to the landless, who too often lack the skills and capital for farming success. Within certain limitations corporations may own farm, timber, and grazing land up to 2,500 hectares. In certain situations foreigners may use land ownership as a basis to acquire shares in a corporation. The concept of *ejidos* (cooperative farms) has been changed. *Ejido* farmers may now own land outright, lease or sell it. Many regulations concerning the production and sale of commodities have been lifted. In taking advantage of these opportunities be sure to get competent legal advice.

Extractive Industries

The great financier, J. P. Getty, once said that "the meek shall inherit the earth but not its mineral rights." Mexicans feel differently. According to the Constitution the subsoil and all its minerals are the inalienable property of the people, national patrimony. In spite of NAFTA primary oil production is still nationalized. Mining requires a government concession. Mexico has one of the world's largest oil reserves. Most of it is located under the plains edging the Gulf of Mexico. It is extremely high quality. Roughly four billion dollars per year is being invested in expansion of PEMEX, the state oil conglomerate. These funds are going for exploration, refining, storage, and transportation. Even with all these expenditures, the Mexican oil and mining industries are probably under invested. Nevertheless, Mexico is the world's largest producer of silver. It is also a world leader in iron ore, copper, lead, zinc, flourite and gold. Some mineral extraction comes from expanded Aztec mines.

Manufacturing

Manufacturing represents about one-fourth of Mexico's gross domestic product. In recent years manufacturing has surpassed oil as the main export.

Manufacturing centers include Mexico City, Monterrey, Guadalajara, and Puebla. Production in border areas such as Tijuana and Ciudad Juárez is rapidly growing. Mexican products range from chemicals and steel to textiles, processed food, construction materials, autos and auto parts, glass, and beer.

Production in Mexico is so cheap and efficient that foreign investors in Mexico produce goods for the entire world, not just Mexico and the United States. Ironically, a few industries, hot house lilies protected too long under Mexico's former import substitution policies, now lack exportability.

Maquiladoras

Mexico's *maquiladoras* are literally "grinding places," foreign-owned production-sharing factories which enjoy tax advantages by bringing U.S. parts across the border to Mexico so cheap Mexican labor can complete assembly for shipment back to the United States. This type of in-bond production is so lucrative that Japan and all four of Korea's conglomerates operate *maquiladoras*. Since their inception in 1965 the *maquiladoras* in the booming border towns of Tijuana, Juárez, and Mexicali have provided badly needed employment and foreign exchange for Mexico. They churn out a wide range of products from automotive to consumer electronics.

Because *maquiladora* workers typically earn eight to twelve dollars per day, the system has made it possible for U.S. industries to compete with low-wage production in Southeast Asia. Asian companies have quickly responded. Hitachi expanded its *maquiladora* color television plant in Tijuana to produce for the Mexican as well as the U.S. market. Taiwanese business interests are organizing an industrial park in Mexicali.

Mexico has over two thousand *maquiladora* plants including almost a thousand in Baja. They employ almost half a million workers and provide a major source of foreign exchange for Mexico. Ciudad Juárez, the cradle of the *maquiladora* system, has over three hundred such plants. Two-thirds of all workers in Juárez depend on *maquiladoras* for employment.

With NAFTA's loosened restrictions on foreign investment and gradual elimination of tariffs, the effectiveness of *maquiladoras* could change. The in-bond program will continue until 2001, at which time value-added is projected to reach twenty billion dollars. Restrictions on sales of *maquiladora* products within Mexico are being eliminated over seven years from the January 1, 1994, effective date of NAFTA. Parts sent for assembly to *maquiladoras* must have an increasing percentage of U.S. or Canadian production to qualify for NAFTA advantages.

During the 1994-2000 transitional period NAFTA allows *maquiladoras* to follow many past practices. Parts can be imported into Mexico duty-free as long as all assembled products are exported from Mexico. Operations can still be fully owned by foreigners. For the transitional period NAFTA rules discard four restrictions pertaining to sales in Mexican markets and drops requirements for positive foreign exchange flows. The total effect is to give *maquiladoras* easier access to Mexican markets.

Other NAFTA changes for *maquiladoras* are also favorable. These involve elimination of quotas and reduction in tariffs for a portion of U.S.-Mexican trade in textiles and apparel. *Maquiladoras* in the automotive industry benefit from new local-content rules. U.S. duties on imports of *maquiladora* products now apply only to third-country components. Duties on Mexican value-added are dropped.

In 2001 NAFTA will apply North American rules of origin for duty exemptions. Imported inputs for *maquiladoras* from outside North America, now exempt, will then be assessed duties. This will have the effect of establishing a barrier to inputs from Europe and Asia. In response overseas firms will likely move production of *maquiladora* inputs to Mexico. By 2001 NAFTA's provisions for freer trade and investment within North America will eliminate the reasons *maquiladoras* exist.

The 1995 peso devaluation helps *maquiladoras* by lowering their labor and service costs (paid in pesos) and increasing the value of sales (paid in dollars). The Mexican competition which sells in pesos and services its debts in dollars, may not survive.

Tourism

Mexico hosts more than seven million tourists per year, most from the United States. This does not include millions of visits by foreigners to Mexico's border areas. A growing number of guests enjoy Mexico's long coasts, lovely bays, colonial Spanish towns, Aztec and Mayan archaeological sites, and luxurious resorts. When the United States is in the grip of Father Frost much of Mexico is warm and sunny. Due to peso devaluations the dollar has considerable buying power.

According to the Mexican Constitution land and buildings within thirty-one miles of the seacoast or sixty-two miles from borders may not be owned by foreigners. This restriction can be partly circumvented by hiring an attorney and placing such property with a Mexican bank as trustee. The trustee holds only the basic title to the property while you as beneficiary retain broad rights for use and development.

There are ample opportunities for foreign investment in the Mexican tourist industry because its growth, while rapid, has been uneven. Hotel construction is booming while secondary tourist facilities, such as golf courses and marinas are developing more slowly.

Banking and Finance

The government-owned central bank, Banco de México, designed to function autonomously within the federal government, sets monetary policy. In recent years the commercial banking system has been largely deregulated and privatized. There are two types of banks: Commercial banks operate much like commercial banks in the United States, handling savings and checking accounts and providing loans for consumers and businesses. Developmental banks serve special purposes by financing projects as diverse as farm operations and housing developments. Many foreign banks now have offices in Mexico. Foreigners may have minority ownership in Mexican banks. Most currency exchange controls have been repealed.

Mexico's Security Markets Law governs the operation of the National Securities Commission, an agency of the Ministry of Finance and Public Credit. Approval of the National Securities Commission is required to list a security on an exchange. Listed companies must issue annual audited and quarterly unaudited financial statements. Mexican auditors and accountants usually maintain high standards.

There is considerable new interest in securities. The rapid increase in issuance of mutual funds has opened stock investing to many small investors. Both trading volume and the issuance of new equities have increased in recent years.

In December 1994 the stock market crashed as a result of a sharp devaluation of the peso. The government's inability to deal with the armed uprising of Mayan Indians in Chiapas was cited as a reason for loss of confidence by investors.

Trade

Two-thirds of total Mexican trade is with the United States. Less than ten per cent of total U.S. trade is with Mexico. However, Mexican trade is important to the United States. Our exports to Mexico are almost as large as our exports to Japan but are growing faster. The United States often has a substantial trade surplus with Mexico compared to chronic large deficits with Japan.

Mexico's exports consist primarily of commodities subject to volatile world prices such as oil, coffee, sugar, and cotton. Much of the foreign exchange earned from these export sales is spent on imported luxury goods by Mexico's rich. The remaining foreign exchange is not enough to cover the cost of importing capital goods such as machine tools, transportation equipment, and heavy machinery. The shortfall was covered by government borrowing abroad. At times such debts were so huge Mexico's questionable ability to pay them threatened the stability of the international financial system. Fortunately for Mexico, NAFTA has switched the emphasis from foreign borrowing by the Mexican government (for state industries) to direct foreign investment (for private industry).

Mexico is deregulating controls on both imports and exports to conform with NAFTA and GATT standards. Foreign companies operating in Mexico can benefit. A substantial portion of Mexico's export of manufactured products is by subsidiaries of multinational companies such as General Motors, Motorola, and Xerox.

Mexico's primary points of entry for foreign trade are Veracruz and Tampico on the Gulf of Mexico, Tijuana and Nuevo Laredo on the northern border, and Acapulco and

Manzanillo on the Pacific Coast. Airports serving foreign trade include Mexico City, Monterrey, and Guadalajara.

NAFTA

In the eighteenth century Adam Smith extolled the virtues of free trade. In it each nation can specialize in goods it can produce better and most cheaply. Thus fewer resources are used in production and consumers everywhere benefit from higher quality and lower prices.

Though free trade is usually a win-win situation, it took a long time for political recognition of this fact. The Smoot-Hawley Act tried to protect the U.S. market from the ravages of the Great Depression by raising tariffs nearly sixty per cent. But other nations retaliated. Within two years U.S. export volume fell by sixty-seven per cent, producing widespread unemployment and devastating entire industries. For the United States, protectionism prolonged and exasperated the Great Depression.

According to the U.S. Department of Commerce the North American Free Trade Agreement, which took effect January 1, 1994, is creating the largest market in the world, a 6.5 trillion dollar market with 370 million people.

The eventual elimination of all tariffs will benefit both the United States and Mexico.

The United States benefits because the Mexican tariffs to be eliminated are 2.5 times U.S. tariffs, thus leveling the playing field. In addition to access to cheap Mexican labor U.S. industries benefit from freedom to enter a Mexican market which is growing much faster than ours. The U.S. benefited from NAFTA before it even went into effect. Shortly after negotiations for this agreement began the chronic U.S. trade deficit with Mexico became a substantial surplus.

Mexico benefits in many ways: expansion of Mexican exports due to gradual elimination of U.S. tariffs, economies of scale in manufacturing by producing for a larger market, increases in employment and foreign investment, expansion of financial and credit markets, and increased automation of production. Mexican agricultural tariffs are reduced in a long fifteen-year phase-out in order to give Mexican farm workers time to adjust. This should reduce the need for displaced Mexican farm workers to migrate to the United States.

NAFTA has more than economic significance for Mexico. It represents a chance for it to modernize its society and enter the contemporary world.

It is important to understand what NAFTA is not. It is not a common market. A common market, such as Europe's, seeks to eliminate restrictions on the movement of labor and capital and tries to coordinate monetary, fiscal, and social policies. Because NAFTA is limited to liberalization of trade and investment, it lacks the problems of a common market.

It is likely that Chile and other Latin American nations will join with NAFTA to create a Western Hemisphere Free Trade Area (WHFTA). According to a study done by the International Institute of Economics, WHFTA would increase U.S. exports to Latin American nations by fifty-one per cent and U.S. imports from Latin America by forty-three per cent.

Economic Prospects

Even with NAFTA a Mexican boom is no certainty. The prospects for the Mexican economy ultimately hinge on the nation's willingness to accept change. Can a modern economy take root in a society which still clings to so many vestiges of a medieval system? The answer cannot be found by compiling economic statistics or constructing models. It involves feelings, habits, and attitudes, the nuts and bolts of culture.

The economic model Mexico is using for development is based on the one used by Taiwan, Korea, and other Asian nations, where new economic systems were successfully grafted to old societies. But Mexico is no Korea or Taiwan. It falls far short of these nations in such critical areas as education, work ethics, savings rates, infrastructure investment, and social cohesion. If Mexico wants to break out of its role as an exporter of low-wage products it will have to change its society to deal with these shortfalls. Simply signing international economic agreements will not suffice, Mexico must muster the will and discipline to take full advantage of such pacts. The sharp devaluation of the peso in December 1994 was an admission that brittle old ways still persist. Now mañana can no longer be postponed.

Recent descriptions in the financial press of Mexico as a Latin American "tiger" or "dragon" are misleading. Its economy is struggling to make progress, like a beast of burden. No dragon, no tiger.

Mexico's economy *is* making progress but it is fraught with problems. We shall look at some of them in the next chapter.

6. Problems

Excess Population

Mexico's burgeoning population produces many problems. A nation burdened by too many children produces too little savings to finance an industrial economy. Social services such as medical clinics and schools cannot keep up. Roads and railroads are jammed. Add the shortage of arable land and you have a recipe for poverty, misery, and emigration of excess people to the United States.

Education

Modern economies require high educational standards. When East Asia was developing in the 1960s, few school-age kids were on the streets nights and weekends because they were attending after-school schools. Those who *were* outside were reading at corner book-rental kiosks. Poor families deprived themselves to send a child to school. School libraries opened at four in the morning. By five they were filled with students. In freezing winter weather they turned the pages with mittens because there was no heat. Many schools taught calculus in the seventh grade.

Mexico lacks this dedication to education. Though compulsory education was extended from six to nine years only half of Mexico's children complete six. Too many school-age children do not go to school at all. They can be seen loitering and roaming the streets in large numbers during school hours. Others help with harvests such as bananas and sugar cane instead of attending school.

What chance does a Mexican who knows only how to harvest crops, grind corn, and shine shoes have to compete with an East Asian kid adept at differential and integral calculus? Modern economies are based on knowledge and applications of disciplines as diverse as topology, real analysis, solid-state physics, biochemistry, computer and material sciences, cost accounting, foreign languages, quality control, production engineering, wire-line skills, digital signal processing, and aerodynamics. Mexican youngsters compete with Asian students who are preparing themselves for such fields ten hours per day, seven days per week, eleven months per year. In the world economy it takes a good education to be a winner.

Pollution

During my trip through Chiapas I saw landscapes denuded by clear-cut logging and strip-mining. In Mexico City the air was so toxic it was almost impossible to breathe. In most of Mexico pollution of air and water is rising in proportion to the increased production of steel, chemicals, and natural resource commodities. Health costs from pollution negate much of the industrial gain.

There are opportunities for U.S. pollution control businesses. NAFTA has environmental requirements. The government is trying to combat pollution by allowing accelerated depreciation of pollution control equipment. Attempts are being made to reform Mexico's environmental protection agency, which lacks both sufficient funding and adequate regulatory power. Meanwhile the bureaucracy drags its heels while seven of every ten babies born in Mexico City suffer toxic blood levels for lead.

Ethnic Minorities

Mexico is not a homogenous nation. About twenty per cent of its population consists of pureblood Indians still in tribal cultures. There are about fifty Indian groups: each has its own language. These range from the Yaqui Indians of the northwest to the Mayas of the Yucatán and the Mixtecs of Oaxaca. Many live in remote forests, deserts or mountains with no road access, no plumbing, no electric power. They are considered backward and are abused by Mexicans with Spanish blood. If not integrated into Mexico's emerging modern economy, these Indians will be economic and political liabilities forever.

There is a hard question Mexico must answer. Why is a nation propelled into the modern world by NAFTA, GATT, and free-market technocrats suddenly rocked by Indians: Mayans, Tzeltzals, Tzotzlales, Tojotavaes, Choles, and others, who rebel with machetes and rusty hunting rifles? Could Mexico disintegrate in ethnic convulsions like Yugoslavia and the former Soviet Union? Your company will expect you to have some answers. The degree of political risk for your business activities can be best determined on the ground, in Mexico.

Drugs

Because some of the illegal narcotics which Mexico produces and transports stick in the pipeline, Mexico also has a drug problem. Bribes from drug merchants to officials subvert the political system. Smugglers too cheap to pay bribes dump their drugs on the Mexican market when they expect arrest.

The relationship between some government officials and the drug kings is insidious. Substantial areas are run by drug lords who are folk heroes for the young and poor. They produce half the marijuana and one-fourth the heroin used in the United States. Cocaine processed in Columbia is also transported north. For a fee the Mexican police sometimes produce videos for television showing narcotics officials burning marijuana fields (after the harvest). This results in good press for the cops and benefits the drug rings by clearing the fields for the next marijuana crop.

Bureaucracy

During a period in which other nations, such as the United States, have reduced their official bureaucracies, Mexico's has grown. Its five million bureaucrats probably have more power than the ruling party. This bureaucracy thrives on inefficiency. By complicating and prolonging government processes it justifies adding new bureaucrats.

Though much of the Mexican economy has been deregulated and privatized, the bureaucracy still creates bottlenecks. It is so slow to change that much Mexican business operates in a free market. In this case "free market" means free of both regulation and taxes.

Much of the old arrogance is still there. In July 1994 Mexico's bureaucracy invaded Wal-Mart's new Supercenter in Mexico City, hauled away products without Spanish labels, and closed the store for three days. Some executives of Kmart, Radio Shack and other corporations complain about mountains of paperwork and arbitrary regulations. All of this violates the spirit of NAFTA.

Many working-level Mexican bureaucrats harbor resentment at Yankee imperialists like you. Too many are primarily interested in transferring "resources" (your money) from "have nations" (such as the United States) to "have-not nations" (such as Mexico). They will be eager to torpedo your business plans. For them, "selling out to gringos" is political suicide.

Corruption

For too much of Mexico's bureaucracy the motto is "don't rock the trough." The Mexican business and economic systems are greased by *la mordida*, "the bite," the bribe. It is so routine that highway police do not bother to concoct phony traffic violations in order to extort bribes. They simply park at certain corners knowing that bus and truck drivers will stop and pay them.

Some police require a tip from victims before investigating crimes. Much of the press is bribed by government; the government, by business. Employees sometimes have to "rent" their jobs from their supervisors. Even poor Indian women have to pay *la mordida* to local police so they can use street corners to sell chewing gum. A corpulent street vendor in Guadalajara, peering up from his viands complained: "If you no pay *mordida, señor*, nothing happen!"

Uprisings

On January 1, 1994, a peasant army of Mayan Indians seized several towns, ranches, and farms in Chiapas. Led by a green-eyed, educated revolutionary known as Subcomandante Marcos, this Zapatista National Liberation Army waged a two-week war in which four hundred people were killed. For a while the Indians occupied much of San Cristobal de las Casas. Tourists were evacuated under armed escort by the Mexican amy. A unit of leftist guerrillas from Central America helped the rebels take the town of Ocosingo.

The spirit of the revolt in Chiapas spread to other parts of Mexico. Thousands marched in support through towns in central and southern Mexico occupying town halls and throwing out local bosses. More than two hundred people were kidnapped. Three car bombs exploded in Mexico City. In Puebla three thousand people formed their own Zapatista unit. Sugar cane workers in Michoacan asked for arms.

There are historical reasons why the revolt originated in Chiapas. Since colonial times it was developed by wealthy cattle ranchers and plantation owners. A few families, using "white terror squads,"suppressed Indian peons in Chiapas and revolutions such as *la Reforma* and *tierra y libertad*.

Ironically, the Mexican government born of revolution underestimated the discontent which caused it. For the Mexican government the Chiapas revolt should be a wake-up call.

But it is not. Mexico's reforms do not benefit everyone. There are winners and losers. The Indians of Chiapas are losers. The 1992 agrarian law which benefits agricultural corporations hurts the small subsistence farmers of Chiapas. This law ends the breakup of large estates into small *ejidos*, permits leasing of small plots to large corporations, and allows large agribusinesses to own large plots of land for the first time since the Mexican Revolution. In Mexico small farmers will be replaced by large agricultural corporations as in the United States.

The people of Chiapas take their problems and the revolt with good humor. In San Cristobal de las Casas I saw cartoon shows on television featuring super-dogs wearing ski masks. A new rock group, the Zapatistas, opened at a local bar wearing big black ski masks. On the streets Indian women hawk cheap dolls wearing tiny black ski masks. If the Mayan Indians of Chiapas could obtain the patents and rights to these, they would be so rich they would have no interest in revolution.

Political Violence

By tradition Mexico uses violence rather than democracy to solve its problems. Many of its leaders were murdered for political reasons. Coups, rebellions, and assassinations are part of the culture. For centuries men on horseback have roused the masses only to exploit them once in power.

In addition to violence against the ruling party (as in Chiapas) there is violence in it and by it. The government itself is responsible for violence. On October 2, 1968, at the time of the Olympics, over three hundred demonstrating students were massacred in the Plaza of Tialteloco in Mexico City. Over a thousand were injured. The event emphasized the inadequacy of Mexico's political system and brought questions such as human rights and political choices to the surface.

During the 1980s, fifty-five members of Mexico's Academy of Human Rights were killed by the government for demonstrating for international standards. In June, 1994,

Mexico's Human Rights Commission reported that "hundreds of Mexicans were still being tortured or murdered every year by police." Some were political prisoners.

The Old Guard of the PRI is being pulled by its heels into the modern era. It responds with violence against those who seek reforms, even members of its own party. Prominent politicians have been assassinated because the Old Guard is alarmed by political and economic changes and bitterly resents its loss of power and prestige: Luis Donaldo Colosio, the PRI's 1994 presidential candidate, the police chief of the city of Tijuana, and Ruiz Massieu, the second ranking official of the PRI. If such violence continues few foreign companies will want to invest in the turmoil. Instead of joining the modern world economy, much of Mexico could mimic the fate of Central America: banana wars and pineapple revolutions.

Illegal Immigration

For many years poor Mexicans have immigrated into the United States. If California's Proposition 187 is successful in denying these illegals jobs, schools, and medical care, many will stay in Mexico where they will foment discontent and rebellion. The safety valve will be closed. In the words of a Mexico City shopkeeper: "When things got rough in the past people went to the United States. Now they will go into the streets."

If the result is a civil war the United States would be the first to suffer. A Mexican civil war could be fought partly in such U.S. cities as Los Angeles, which has the world's second largest Mexican population next to Mexico City. The United States could be flooded with a tidal wave of refugees. The long common border could become a war zone. The flow of critical Mexican oil to the United States could stop and U.S. businesses in Mexico could be threatened. Next to Japan, Mexico probably has more impact on the United States than any other nation.

Dependence on the United States

The Mexican economy is too dependent on the United States. Recession in the United States can bring depression in Mexico. During World War II and the early 1950s, the United States dominated Mexican trade almost to the extent of being its only trading partner. Today many Mexican exporters know only the U.S. market. Much of the Mexican economy is designed to serve it. Trade with the United States represents two-thirds of Mexico's total.

The United States, in turn, is dependent upon foreigners, who hold roughly a third of the foreign debt. If bond traders, particularly Japanese, fail to rollover their investments at U.S. bond auctions, U.S. interest rates could soar, adding over a billion dollars a year to Mexico's debt service for each percentage point of increase.

Devaluation

In December 1994 the peso lost forty per cent of its value. Prices plunged faster than currency dealers could post new prices under *compra* (buy) and *venta* (sell). Long lines of Mexicans trying to exchange pesos for dollars recalled the 1980s, the decade of devaluation, when the peso plummeted from twelve to three thousand for the dollar. With devaluation came inflation. In one year, 1987, the inflation rate soared 170 per cent.

The fall out was immediate. Foreign investments in Mexico, which had previously helped cover trade deficits, declined. Inflation accelerated. Prices of imported goods such as cars and appliances rose sharply. Mobs converged on currency exchanges to change pesos into dollars. Mexican shoppers disappeared from U.S. border towns. Illegal immigration into the United States increased. On the Balsa stock prices fell sharply triggering huge drops in all other Latin American exchanges. International investors again wondered whether decrepit Latin American social and political systems were capable of accepting modern economies.

On an individual level the devaluation dashed countless hopes and dreams. A youth told me he could no longer plan to attend Michigan State University for an engineering degree because his father's savings, in pesos, had lost forty per cent of its dollar values.

The government blamed the monetary fiasco on a world-wide rise in interest rates, huge trade deficits from the previous (Salinas) administration and the revolt in Chiapas.

The devaluation of the peso increases prices of foreign products in Mexico. Without such price competition prices of domestic goods increase. This inflation leads to higher interest rates which reduce foreign investment, increase the trade deficit, and produce additional peso devaluations. Thus arises the ghost of a familiar and lethal cycle which most economists had declared dead.

Disparity of Income

A rising tide does not lift all boats. Some capsize. While the top fifth of Mexicans achieve first-world incomes, the bottom half remains mired in the mud of the third world. A veneer of jet set opulence covers crushing poverty. Real estate prices boom in Puerto Vallarta as poor Indians rampage in Chiapas.

The success of the top group creates increased hopes for the rest. Mexicans, like people everywhere, raise their expectations faster than their means. A wizened and dyspeptic shop owner in Guadalajara told me he could remember when few of his neighbors had telephones and television. Now that these were common, "those who don't have them are very impatient."

A nation can not be successful if only an elite is successful. It takes a large number of people with purchasing power to create the demand for mass production which makes an economy spin.

The Challenge of Change

Even though Mexico is rich in resources and hard-working people, it has been unable to join the first-world economy. One is forced to find the reason for this failure by examining its archaic social and political systems.

Time may show that Mexicans are not willing to pay the cultural costs of competing in the world economy. There is mounting evidence that economic changes have already been too sweeping and rapid for the culture to absorb.

The government is having diffficulty wrestling with the problem of balancing competing foreign and domestic demands. In 1995 the Mexican government was faced with a dilemma. The U.S. government wanted Mexico to put up its oil reserves as collateral for a loan to protect the peso. Oil and minerals have always been considered a sacred part of the national patrimony in Mexico. A government which surrenders valuables under the soil could end up there itself. Foreign investors and governments are requiring Mexico to tighten its austerity belt in return for loans. It is questionable whether the average Mexican, long suffering and long squeezed, has the capacity for additional sacrifice.

Many of Mexico's problems can be traced to the ruling party, which refuses to allow other parties a chance to solve problems. These are numerous: poor infrastructure, political and monetary discipline; political instability; inadequate controls on population growth and pollution; no solutions for bureaucracy, corruption and drugs; no answers for unemployment and inflation.

7. Doing Business in Mexico

Opportunities and Risks

Considering the problems addressed in the last chapter, how should Americans do business in Mexico? The answer: very carefully! There are both advantages and disadvantages. Advantages include incentives under NAFTA, potential profits higher than in the United States, and cheaper labor. Disadvantages include differences in cultures, language and legal systems; poor infrastructure, credit difficulties, extensive pollution, high crime rates, fast labor turnover, and a shortage of experienced mid-level managers.

The U.S. Embassy in Mexico City produces lists of the best business opportunities. These include projected growth rates for industries and sectors within industries. Recent lists featured double-digit annual growth projections in the automotive, computer, communications, engineering, pollution control, financial services, hotel and restaurant industries. Private business research organizations have indicated huge demand for low-cost housing, machine tools, and agricultural machinery. When developing business plans for Mexico be sure to obtain the most recent lists of opportunities generated by both public and private agencies.

Business Laws

Mexican business laws, including those relating to foreign investment, intellectual property protection, transfer of technology, and income and value-added taxes are federal not state. Regulations are constantly changing. Always obtain professional legal advice.

A 1989 law loosened restrictions on foreign investment, allowing 100% foreign ownership in many industries. Exceptions include petroleum, some primary petrochemicals, gas distribution, some communications, forestry, and certain transportation systems. These require prior approval of the Foreign Investment Commission. Applicants must show their investments will benefit the Mexican economy. Approval of applications for most projects are deemed automatic if regulatory agencies fail to decide within ninety days. New procedures were instituted to encourage foreign investment through stock exchanges.

A 1990 law allows private ownership of banks but not controlling ownership by foreigners. In industries where full foreign ownership is permitted no prior governmental approval is needed as long as the project adheres to environmental rules, keeps imports and exports in balance the first three years, uses updated technology, is located outside Mexico City, Guadalajara, or Monterrey (if an industrial operation), and is capitalized with foreign funds not exceeding one hundred million dollars. The Ministry of Foreign Affairs states it will register the investment and authorize property acquisitions for such projects within a few months.

A 1991 law protects property through patents, trademarks, and copyrights. Patent periods were extended from fourteen to twenty years and were expanded to a wider variety of processes and products. Trademarks can be renewed for ten year periods. There are provisions for criminal and civil penalties for infringements.

The Mexican government wants to encourage investment of foreign capital. For this it relies on normal market attractions rather than government subsidies as incentives. Almost the only tax break applied to encourage foreign investment is the possibility of accelerated depreciation for plant modernization and renewal. At the present time there are no restrictions on repatriation of capital or profits.

For professional up-to-date advice on Mexican business law and accounting practices obtain a copy of *Doing Business in Mexico* from Price Waterhouse or contact one of their Mexican offices.

Taxes

Mexico is not a tax haven. Though there are no state or local taxes on corporate earnings, the tax burden in Mexico is roughly equivalent to other nations.

Traditionally Mexican businesses complied poorly with tax requirements. Only foreign businesses paid in full. Mexican businesses looked at government tax auditors as people who arrived after the battle and bayoneted the wounded. Many could be bribed.

All of this changed in the first year of the Salinas administration, which launched a tax-compliance bloodbath. After a campaign involving special audits, prosecutions, imprisonments, beatings, torture sessions, and other draconian measures, Mexico's faint-hearted managers fully complied. By 1991 official tax terrorism had expanded the base sufficiently to reduce the corporate rate to thirty-five per cent. Mexico now exchanges tax information with the United States government. Punishment for avoidance is severe. There are no tax holidays.

Federal taxes apply to income, imports and exports, value-added transactions and payrolls. Local taxes are levied on real property and salaries. Non-resident taxpayers (including corporations) are taxed only on Mexican income; resident taxpayers (including corporations) are taxed on worldwide income. Corporate income is taxed at the corporate level only. Dividends are not subject to tax until they exceed net after-tax earnings. Capital gains are included in gross income. There is a minimum corporate tax based on assets. Compulsory profit-sharing, amounting to ten per cent of adjusted taxable income, is payable annually to employees. It is partly tax deductible.

Mexico provides a tax incentive to exporters by eliminating the value-added tax (VAT) for exporters and allowing a refund or credit on VAT charges by others for goods or services used in the production of exports. Limited tax credits may be granted for foreign taxes paid according to international tax treaties.

The above information should be used only as a starting point. It is sure to change. For the most recent information seek professional help by using references listed in chapters nine, thirteen, and fourteen.

Effects of NAFTA and GATT

For centuries Mexican businesses felt secure behind high tariff barriers. Mexico was a sleepy captive market so there was no need for quality control or marketing. Long-established connections ensured steady sales and high mark-ups, producing huge profits on low volumes.

This closed system has been shattered by NAFTA and GATT. Competition, a concept alien to many Mexicans, is now essential for success. To win today Mexican companies must provide high-quality goods, low prices, prompt delivery, and efficient service. Mexico's paramount cultural value of amenity is melting in the crucible of competition. In the past Mexicans have quit rather than endure competitive work situations which most U.S. workers thrive on and enjoy. It will be interesting to see how Mexican companies and employees respond to the profound changes wrought by GATT and NAFTA.

According to a U.S. Department of Commerce report American companies are benefiting greatly from NAFTA. Industries which especially benefit include processed foods, textiles, motor vehicles, auto parts, and appliances. Mexican consumers prefer these U.S. products over their own. The growing Mexican population is increasing demand for U.S. building materials, construction goods, and household furniture. Lower tariffs are helping sales of U.S. semiconductors, pharmaceuticals, computer equipment, telecommunications, aerospace, photographic, medical, and petroleum-refining equipment; and air conditioning, refrigeration, and heating machinery. U.S. services such as banking, construction, financing, and insurance are prospering in Mexico. In most industries Mexican demand is increasing seven to ten times as fast as in the United States. The voracious Mexican demand for U.S. goods was a key cause of the Mexican deficit and loss of foreign reserves which led to the January 1995 devaluation of the peso. It was simply too much, too fast.

NAFTA gives U.S. businesses an edge over Asian and European competitors because it requires substantial North American labor and material input for a product to qualify for trade advantages. As an example television picture tubes and computer motherboards must be built in the United States or Canada to qualify for reduced Mexican tariffs. U.S. employment is growing because U.S. firms no longer need to manufacture in Mexico to avoid high Mexican tariffs.

NAFTA eliminates U.S., Mexican, and Canadian tariffs for most products and knocks down investment restrictions over a ten to fifteen year period. The list of winners is long: GM, Ford, Chrysler, Kodak, Xerox, Proctor and Gamble, Gillette, Nike, many banks and insurance companies and many medium and small-sized businesses. The list of losers is short: winter fruit and vegetable producers and sugar growers. NAFTA is such a powerful magnet it is pulling in capital from outside the continent. Japanese banks, resort operators, and auto producers are investing heavily in Mexico. Taiwanese investors are developing an industrial park in Mexicali. The influx of capital is producing better employment opportunities for Mexicans and may reduce illegal immigration to the United States.

Maquiladoras

Mexico's duty-free assembly plants, called *maquiladoras*, now number over two thousand and employ about half a million workers. With the devaluation of the peso the average worker's wage has slipped from $2.50 per hour to less than $2.00, attracting companies from as far away as Germany, Korea, and Taiwan. The roster of *maquiladora* companies reads like a *Who's Who* of international business: Siemens, Sony, Philips, General Motors and all four major Korean conglomerates. Smaller suppliers are now establishing *maquiladoras* in order to provide just-in-time parts to large manufacturers.

If you are considering establishing a *maquiladora* you might contact Grupo Bermudaz in Ciudad Juárez, or one of the shelter companies, such as Cal Pacifico, which arrange *maquiladora* operations. Information on these companies is included in chapters nine and thirteen.

Maquiladoras allow you to ship parts from the United States, assemble them in Mexico, and pay customs duties only on the non-U.S. value added. These duties are diminishing in accordance with NAFTA. *Maquiladora* managers told me their Mexican plants were 25% more productive than their U.S. plants. Under certain circumstances *maquiladoras* may be 100% owned by foreigners.

Maquiladoras have dulled the gaudy luster of Mexico's border towns. Tijuana, the city where Margarita Cansino became Rita Hayworth, where half the World War II female population worked as sexual barnacles, is now a hard-driving industrial center which gets up too early to party.

In February 1995 the Mexican government eliminated a tax break for *maquiladoras*, forcing them to report their dealings with U.S. parent companies as if they were transactions with unrelated businesses. These increased Mexican taxes are partly balanced by U.S. tax credits but costs for accounting and tax preparation went up. So did the required payment of ten per cent of profits to employees. The new laws are complicated. Seek the advice of a law firm situated in Mexico, such as Baker and McKenzie.

Shelter Companies

Cal Pacifico of California, Baja California's oldest *maquiladora* shelter operator, is a fine example of a shelter operation. Since 1966 it has helped companies establish and administer operations in Mexico. It performs administrative, human resources, financial, and export/import details of operations so clients can concentrate on production. Economies of scale allow it to provide services for less than it would cost a small firm. Its clients range from assemblers of medical equipment, electronic components, aircraft parts, television sets, and telephone equipment to manufacturers of window coverings, leather goods, and sports equipment.

Cal Pacifico provides everything for a company's Mexican operation except technical know-how, capital equipment, and raw materials. They find and lease a building and help with tenant improvements. They obtain Mexican permits; help recruit, interview, and hire employees: handle payroll, accounting, bookkeeping, employee benefits and taxes. As a licensed U.S. customs broker they arrange U.S. imports. They provide movement of freight to and from Mexico and obtain Mexican immigration visas for non-resident employees and visitors. Cal Pacifico provides basic employee medical care, buys local supplies, and arranges for services such as power, water, electricity, communications, security, and maintenance.

TraTec of California, located in Chula Vista, stresses cultural sensitivity as a key but often ignored factor in the planning stages and ultimate success of a *maquiladora*. TraTec offers a wide range of services. These include *maquiladora* access, contract manufacturing, and turnkey operations. TraTec's advantages include elimination of large capital outlays, Mexican incorporations, long-term contracts, and long start-up schedules. TraTec's services extend to Tijuana, Tecate, Nogales, Hermosillo, and Ciudad Obregon.

Addresses for TraTec and Cal Pacifico are in chapter thirteen.

Establishing a Business

If you are thinking of establishing a business in Mexico, you picked a good time. The role of business is changing more rapidly than any time since the revolution. Due to the global collapse of communism, business, for the first time, is recognized as a powerful force in the development of a nation. Mexico's future will be determined largely by the ability of business to manage and risk change.

To be accepted in Mexico your business will have to show less concern with short-term profits and more interest in long-term benefits for Mexican employees, customers, and shareholders. The new rules for business require commitment; one can no longer "take the money and run." Only win-win visionaries will succeed.

To form a business in Mexico you will need competent legal, accounting, and tax advice early in the process. Prior approval of the Minister of Foreign Affairs is required to form a corporation or any business entity. Though there are nine forms of business enterprises, the most common form of foreign investment is corporate, permitting a firm to add *S.A.* (*Sociedad Anómina*) after its name. Corporations with variable capital are designated *S.A. de C.V.* Corporations involving foreign capital are designated *S. en N.C.* for general partnerships and *S. de R.L.* for limited partnerships. Mexican attorneys can form corporations in about a month at reasonable costs. All shares must be registered.

Management

Too many Mexican managements stick to outmoded ways. They harbor paternalistic fears of delegating authority and feel threatened by the initiatives of employees. They value nepotism over quality control and efficiency, security over challenge, effete intellectualism over practical solutions, and verbal intentions over concrete accomplishments. When all is said and done more is said than done.

You will need to change all this by developing modern participatory management systems, teaching workers educated with too much theory how to apply knowledge to practical problem solving and decision-making, and introducing time management to a mañana society. This will not be easy.

You will have to differentiate Mexican cultural practices which cannot be changed from those which must be changed to run a modern business. The cultures are very different. Mexicans feel little urgency; in the U.S. time is vital. Mexicans learn by rote; Americans, by questioning. In Mexico families come before jobs; in the United States one must "go an extra mile for the company." Mexicans place politeness over truth; in the United States the truth hurts. Mexicans consider manual labor demeaning; in the United States wealthy people often work at ceramics, gardening, or woodworking as hobbies. A young Mexican man I met on the train from Mexico City exemplified such cultural conflict. He had delivered pizza for an American company and was a highly-rated employee. Then he took two weeks off to go to a family wedding. Upon his return he was fired because he had not worked long enough to earn vacation days. He did not understand why he was fired because his behavior was typically Mexican.

Teamwork and Competition

You will need to develop teamwork since Mexicans are accustomed to working in a superior/subordinate structure which resembles a paternalistic father-child relationship. In this hierarchy quality of work is not a factor. Mutual obligations are medieval. The patron relieves the serf of decisions and hands out favors in return for respect and loyalty. This vertical structure is no longer accepted by modern companies which have been flattening their structures for decades. You should replace this hierarchy with a system of teamwork based on family values honored bv all Mexicans. Then you will have self-disciplining efficiency and fewer absentees. Teamwork is especially important because Mexican workers will not compete with each other. When pushed to compete they are likely to quit rather than break the Mexican custom of amenability.

Problem Solving

A typical Mexican response to a problem is to delay and avoid it. Problems will be reported to you too late to resolve but in sufficient time to blame someone else. As an act of loyalty your workers will improvise solutions which raise costs and lower quality.

You can improve problem solving skills by instilling accountability, clarifying goals, and encouraging participation in pre-task planning and post-task critiques. Take a proactive stance by identifying problems before they become too serious. Try an anonymous suggestion box, bonuses for productive ideas, and holding teams responsible for efficiency and quality control. Get out of your office and walk through every nook and cranny. Ask all your people hard questions.

Priorities

Mexicans tend to give priorities to the most recent assignments. They raise the importance of tasks which relate to their own job performances rather than those which benefit the company as a whole. You need to clearly communicate priorities of tasks, perhaps by assigning due dates to designate order of completion.

Evaluation and Promotion

In the past promotions have been based on family and friendship connections. Loyalty took precedence over ability. A promoted Mexican could not act like his job performance earned him the promotion because it probably did not. Mexicans who do not have connections often prefer to work for U.S. companies because they know they will be evaluated on merit.

Training

Mexican law requires all businesses to devote a portion of their resources to training employees. Yet many U.S. executives told me Mexico had too many *untrained* workers. What is wrong? Training is often so theoretical it fails in practice. The application of new skills is often ignored. Above all, training often fails because it ignores Mexican cultural assumptions. Appropriate well-developed training programs pay for themselves with better quality and productivity, improved work environments, and better job satisfaction.

Accounting

Mexico has professional accounting standards. The title of *contador público*, public accountant, is granted to qualifying college graduates, who are allowed to use the intitials *C.P.* after their names.

Accounting and auditing procedures are roughly similar to those in the United States. Basic financial statements include the balance sheet, income statement, changes in stockholders' equity, and changes in financial position. Due to Mexico's history of rapid inflation financial statements should be carefully restated to reflect its effects.

Marketing and Advertising

Much of the Mexican market, at least the under half in income, is fascinated by pop culture trends in the United States. It loves Levis, Cokes, fast foods and rock music.

Franchises are very popular in Mexico. If you consider one be sure it sells something different and does not compete with better and cheaper local products.

American marketers in Mexico cautioned me against direct mail campaigns. The Mexican mail system is too slow and undependable.

Advertisers must understand the culture. A U.S. auto called the "Caliente" caused an uproar. For tens of millions of potential buyers "caliente" means "hooker" or "sexual heat."

Labor and Labor Laws

The Mexican labor force is very young. With sufficient training it does a good job. Turnover is fast; some employers reported an annual rate of sixty-five per cent.

Mexican labor law favors employees and unions. Some employers told me they had more problems with competing unions than with management-labor relations.

The average hourly base pay of Mexican workers is under two dollars. But fringe benefits, including pensions, medical costs, profit-sharing, and social security can double or triple hourly wages. By law workers must be paid 365 days per year, including seven paid holidays and a special holiday every six years when a new president is inaugurated. Many businesses also observe religious holidays. Ten per cent of adjusted taxable profits must be distributed to employees. There are labor laws relating to equal opportunities, health and safety, and termination of employment. In some industries employers are expected to provide housing.

Some companies go beyond the laws, giving bags of food to employees who show up to work on time and cash payments to workers who do not extend their weekends by taking Mondays off, which they jestingly call *San Lunes*, "Saint Monday holidays."

8. Bargaining

Is Bargaining Necessary?

Not every problem should be negotiated. Conflict and competition are intrinsic aspects of doing business. If your business is doing well, it may be best not to negotiate small problems. If you have a big advantage over your counterpart, it may be possible to gain concessions by intimidation rather than negotiation. Most of us have friends or spouses who have won personal disputes by refusing to "talk about it."

For negotiations to succeed there are three prerequisites: a negotiable issue, some willingness to compromise, and trust. A *partial* overlap of interests is essential. If the interests of both parties *completely* overlap, no negotiations are needed. If there is *no* overlap, negotiations are futile.

Preparation

A smart negotiator starts before the other side knows it is involved. So kickoff the ball before your Mexicans know the game has started. Quietly gather information about your Mexican counterparts: their business, government, industry, competition, culture, business system, prices, suppliers, and technical capabilities.

Look first at needs. Can you identify the needs of Mexican counterparts? What would they give up to fill these needs? Then define *your* needs. Do you want to form a strategic alliance, establish manufacturing or distribution centers, enter new markets, make an acquisition, or satisfy increased consumer demand? Quantify your expected investment and returns.

Make a list of information needed to ask appropriate questions. Separate facts from assumptions. List concessions you can grant the other side without hurting yours. Establish your company's walkaway point, strategy, and ploys.

Mexicans are very concerned about status. Be sure first contact with your Mexican counterparts is not made by a low-level manager, even if that person is most technically competent.

Organizing the Negotiating Team

Your team will vary in size depending on the importance of the negotiation. It should be at least as large as the Mexican side. Duties should be assigned to each member. In a small team each member can have several duties.

Your team leader should have an important title and high status. This person should keep the talks on track, signal breaks for team conferences, and lead strategy sessions.

Choose a technical representative who can clearly explain the capabilities and limitations of your product or service without revealing too much proprietary information.

Your legal representative may be your corporate lawyer or an attorney familiar with Mexican law. The International Trade Administration maintains lists of competent lawyers who specialize in foreign law.

Some teams include a speaker and a listener/recorder. The speaker serves as the single voice of the team for private negotiations and public announcements. The listener/recorder notes all verbal and symbolic Mexican statements.

The logistics coordinator is responsible for materials, travel, and communication. This person might arrive in Mexico a few days early to confirm hotel, travel, and restaurant reservations; check arrival of materials and mail, and coordinate the agenda and itinerary with the Mexican side.

Your translator will be a key member. This person should serve as cultural advisor to the leader and conduct language and cultural training for the team. This should include team practice in showing Mexican-style deference to your team leader. It will likely be a pleasant change for that person!

Someone will have to be responsible for finances and crunching numbers: paying bills, maintaining payroll and ensuring the terms of the final contract satisfy financial goals.

Avoid frequent changes of team members. Negotiations for Mexicans are personal. It takes time to develop friendships.

Getting to Know You

Mexico is still a traditional society. Business is centered on contacts and connections based on trust. Mexican business people need to establish trust through personal relationships with potential partners, customers, and suppliers. These often involve slow social relationships so both parties can develop mutual confidence. For Mexicans trust thus formed can be stronger than loyalty to one's company.

Many U.S. business people are reluctant to admit the value of connections because they take so much time and trouble to develop. Mexicans have no such problem. They freely admit who you know is more important than what you know. A trusted contact is more likely to win a contract than an unknown low bidder. For Mexicans human relationships are key to all transactions; at all times, at every level.

Protocol and Etiquette

For Mexicans good etiquette is proof of good breeding. There are standard norms of behavior at and between all levels of society. Class differences are distinct. Mexican managers are not likely to drink beer and throw horseshoes with employees at the company picnic. Do not expect them to don Levis for informal foolishness with the troops. Authority figures must look and act the part.

Because Mexican culture stresses personal dignity, all but the poorest Mexicans dress up rather than down: clean, pressed suits, shined shoes for men; tasteful manicures, high heels and makeup for women; carefully groomed hair and appropriate jewelry for both sexes.

In conversation Mexicans stand much closer than people in the United States. You will feel uncomfortable when your Mexican counterpart stands very close to you. But, if you move back, your Mexican will think you are being aloof.

The customs of gift giving and thank you notes are not as entrenched in Mexico as in the United States. Nevertheless, Mexicans appreciate such small niceties. Do not bring yellow flowers, Mexico's color for mourning.

It is better to talk about innocuous subjects like weather and travel than "wetbacks" and the U.S. war with Mexico. Some Mexicans object to the use of *American* to mean people in the United States. They also consider themselves Americans.

Introductions

Team leaders usually handle introductions at the first negotiating session. Juniors are introduced to seniors as in the United States. A woman must offer her hand before a hand-shake. Men who are long-time friends may embrace in an *abrazo*. Learn some basic greetings in Spanish. Use the formal *usted* address rather than the informal *tu*. Use titles frequently. You may find Mexicans in border areas to be more informal but let such informality develop slowly.

Entertaining

In Mexico the person who offers the entertaining pays expenses: no Dutch treat, no separate checks. Mexican hosts and hostesses have total obligations to their guests. Doing things for yourself, such as fixing yourself a drink or hanging up your coat might imply your host or hostess is negligent. Do not bring a potluck casserole or peek in the refrigerator.

Mexican business meals may last four hours and include several cocktails, wine, a four-course meal, sweet dessert, and cognac. Such meals are intended to cement personal relationships as well as do business.

Time

Time is warped south of the Grande. The Creator made many mañanas for Mexicans. In Mexico it is better to take time to smell the flowers than obey the clock. Only the most vital events start promptly: religious rites, artistic performances, medical appointments. Most events involving time are considered outside human control. Your Mexican counterparts will have trouble organizing time, fulfilling deadlines, and keeping appointments. You should not take these faults as seriously as you would in the United States. Take heart. Mexicans are improving their sense of time . . . but *slowly.*

Publicity and Secrecy

In Mexico both government and business negotiators use special funds to pay reporters to slant news in their favor. News media in the United States often pick up these stories and publish them without checking validity. Sometimes Mexican media are financially induced *not* to cover certain negotiations. Your agreement can be quickly scuttled by muckrakers baiting the Colossus of the North. One article in the press accusing your Mexican counterparts of "selling out to gringos" may end negotiations.

Your negotiations will not go far in the spotlight of press attention. If you receive favorable coverage your Mexicans will think you manipulated the press as they do. So take care to respect confidentiality. Terms and conditions can be more flexible when neither side needs to worry about losing face over concessions. With confidentiality tacit understandings can easily be withdrawn and problems are easier to discuss.

Mexicans maintain a huge gap between rhetoric and reality. In the 1970s and 1980s trade and debt negotiations with the United States were falsely influenced by exaggerated figures for "new, large, proven oil reserves." Prior to the 1995 collapse of the peso wild figures were released pertaining to the size of Mexico's foreign exchange reserves. More than once, Mexican officials have "cried wolf," implying the death of the world financial system if Mexico were denied large, quick loans.

Mexican Neotiating Behavior

Because the Mexican bargaining record has been quite dismal, Mexicans sometimes feel fear when dealing with U.S. negotiators. Past bargaining has not been "win-win" but "win-lose" with Mexicans usually losers. Delays may be manufactured because your Mexican counterparts will not be in a hurry to lose. On the other hand the act of negotiating can be more important for Mexicans than the results. In Mexico prolonged negotiations are better than confrontations which can become violent very easily. So expect your Mexican counterparts to listen, defer comment, and show up late. As the process drags out, do not fidget or focus impatiently on your watch. This is rude in a society which places politeness above efficiency.

When you finally reach an agreement, there will be additional delays. It will take time for your counterparts to obtain approval of higher authorities. For the same reason you should not press your counterpart for quick or sweeping decisions.

Strategy

Some Mexican negotiators are very realistic in determining strategy. They do not adhere to routine negotiating phases such as opening moves, assessment, closure, and implementation. If dealing from weakness, they can be reasonable; if from strength, intractable. Study your counterpart's behavior; then analyze its meaning.

Your strategy will likely follow a four-phase pattern: setting the tone, establishing a bargaining range, negotiating within this range (perhaps by linking concessions), and creating an agreement or walkaway crisis.

In setting the tone take a *we* attitude. Avoid detail. Describe the best possible mutual benefits. Stress common interests and areas of agreement rather than problems and differences.

Then determine the outer limits of the range within which an agreement is possible. Start from an initial position from which you can make fairly large concessions. Movement to agreement can start slowly by linking small concessions. When both teams consist of expert negotiators, they will often send subtle signals to each other expressing their maximum and minimum expectations. This allows time to concentrate on the logistical and technical details necessary to implement the agreement.

Some negotiators start by offering a small concession to show good will. Others prefer to play a waiting game, believing that offering too much, too soon, simply increases the expectations of the other side. They think concessions are not appreciated unless won through hard bargaining. Pairing concessions often works well: "We could probably agree on this issue if we could get the other one right."

Ploys are devices to influence bargaining. They can be positive or negative, clean or dirty, quick or prolonged, but they must fit into strategy and be appropriate to intended goals. There are many ploys: hypothetical (bait) offers, creating a sticky commitment for the other side, playing your counterparts against each other, creating artificial discord, dead horsing (using the other side's culture, goals, systems, or limitations to your advantage), floating decoy rumors, instigating fear and cooperation, creating band-wagon effects, phony language "difficulties," or false deadlines; timing outside events (such as severe price drops) for shock effects, playing status games, and setting up straw man proposals too outrageous for acceptance in order to gain acceptance of slightly less outrageous proposals.

Coming to Agreement

If you have maintained a close relationship with your Mexican counterparts, the shape of an agreement will likely emerge. In the final stage both sides will try to close. Tension may be high at this time because both sides have invested much time, energy, and money. As both sides seek approval of higher authorities, use the time to circulate copies of the prospective contract to concerned departments of your company.

When a complete agreement is not possible and outside events are working in your favor, settle for what is possible and let the outside events settle the rest.

The Contract

An expert negotiator often bargains with a final contract hidden in a pocket or briefcase. This person knows it is important for both parties to agree on a common concept of settlement before becoming embroiled in the minutia of grammar and syntax. Otherwise conflicts will arise over words rather than issues.

Mexican and U.S. contract laws are very different. Be sure your contract states which laws will be applied. Mexico applies the law of nominal value, meaning the price in the contract must be honored. Mexican contract law does not recognize the principle of *rebus sic stantibus*, factual circumstances which might permit a change of contract.

In common law countries such as the United States, a contract can be modified if it is proven that the factual circumstances have altered in a way that burdens one party so much that it is unable to honor the contract. For example, the January 1995 devaluation of the peso by forty per cent produced valid reasons for adjustments of contracts under U.S. but not Mexican law. Changes in circumstances may involve the complex relationship between Mexican business and government. The terms of certain payments required to win official approval of contracts or bypass regulations may be changed by petty government functionaries. For this reason many Mexicans consider their government cumbersome. They try to "beat the system." One who cooperates with authorities is considered a traitor or a snitch.

For specific situations you should always contact an attorney specializing in Mexican-U.S. business law.

Limiting Risk

Your contract should anticipate problems such as poor compliance and stipulate penalties. Performance contracts are often better than set fees. When possible reciprocal performances should be simultaneous. Take care in sharing technology, particularly premature transfer of copyrights and patents.

Financial risks can be limited by reducing the size of the investment. Consider beginning with a final assembly operation and delaying full production and technology transfer until you have scouted all the pitfalls. Avoid extending too much credit. Consider a countertrade deal. Try test marketing your product or service through a performance contract with a Mexican distributor. Avoid contracts which are too comprehensive. Above all, obtain competent legal advice.

9. *How to Get Help*

Sources of Help

Sources of help include U.S. government agencies located in the United States and Mexico, Mexican government agencies located in the United States and Mexico, and private organizations in both countries.

Some U.S. firms seem reluctant to use U.S. government help. Perhaps they fear red tape. Yet the information and services available from the U.S. government are timely, thoroughly researched, and often free.

Addresses and phone numbers of agencies and firms listed here are located in chapter thirteen.

GOVERNMENT AGENCIES

The International Trade Administration

The International Trade Administration, an agency of the Department of Commerce, is organized into trade development sections specializing in such industry sectors as capital goods, consumer goods, transportation, and industrial goods and services. Its staff includes experts on Mexico. The International Trade Administration offers assistance ranging from export mailing lists to product marketing services.

The U.S. and Foreign Commercial Service

The U.S. and Foreign Commercial Service is an arm of the Department of Commerce. It was created to help American business export. US&FCS maintains the commercial library at the U.S. Trade Center in Mexico City. This library covers almost every aspect of doing business in Mexico. Other services include private counseling, arranging appointments with prospects, surveying potential sales representatives, and arranging office services, office space, and market research.

US&FCS produces *World Traders Data Reports* which provide confidential background on possible foreign trading partners, buyers, distributors and retailers. It also furnishes *Export Contact Lists* and the Trade Opportunities Program. US&FCS maintains the *National Trade Data Bank* in CD-ROM at depository libraries around the United States. These include many documents related to Mexico and more than thirty on NAFTA.

The Department of Commerce

The Department of Commerce has a marketing manager for Mexico who assists U.S. firms. Commerce publishes *Market Share Reports* which describe foreign markets. Its Office of Major Contracts assists U.S. firms in obtaining large foreign contracts. Statistical data on trade with Mexico is detailed in *United States Trade with Major Trading Partners*. Upon request Commerce will send you a copy of the *North American Free Trade Agreement* (NAFTA).

The Agency for International Development

The Agency for International Development provides feasibility funding for trade contracts and investments abroad. It also supports banks which finance joint American and foreign ventures.

The Export-Import Bank

The Export-Import Bank develops U.S. export potential by encouraging small and medium-sized businesses. It offers an array of loans, guarantees, and insurance programs. The Foreign Credit Insurance Corporation acts as an agent for the Export-Import Bank to insure U.S. exporters against non-payment by foreign buyers. An example of Ex-Im Bank's programs is the 1994 memorandum of understanding with Banco Nacional De Obras Y Servicios Publicos (the national development bank of Mexico) to help Mexico comply with the requirements of NAFTA by supporting sales of environmental goods and services by U.S. firms to Mexico.

The Small Business Administration

The Small Business Administration guarantees export financing and is structured to meet the needs of the small business owner who plans to enter export markets for the first time. The SBA operates both management and financial assistance programs. It helps connect U.S. exporters with foreign buyers.

The SBA sponsors counseling services through SCORE (Service Corps of Retired Executives). SCORE publishes *Opportunity in Mexico*, an excellent guide to Mexico for small business.

The SBA also provides a free initial consultation with an international trade attorney in conjunction with the Federal Bar Association.

The State Department

The State Department publishes bulletins which provide market leads. State's Office of Business and Export Affairs publishes information on strategies and risk evaluation for U.S. businesses considering Mexican operations.

The Library of Congress

The Library of Congress maintains a special section devoted to foreign laws.

U.S. Embassy and Consulates in Mexico

The U.S. Embassy and consulates in Mexico, through the office of the U.S. Trade Representative, provide feasibility funding for trade, contracts, and investments in Mexico. They also publish information on commercial treaties and trade problems. The U.S. Embassy's economic section provides information on the Mexican economy and the Foreign Agricultural Service furnishes data on Mexican agriculture.

State and Local Governments

Many states, counties, and cities now offer programs to assist firms in international business. Often they sponsor trade missions to Mexico.

PRIVATE AMERICAN ORGANIZATIONS

Dun and Bradstreet

Dun and Bradstreet issues *Private International Businesses* which lists credit information on over fifty thousand firms in over a hundred nations.

U.S. Attorneys Specializing in Foreign Law

You will need the professional help of attorneys for such tasks as obtaining licenses and dealing with Mexican laws. A list of attorneys who specialize in foreign law may be obtained from the International Trade Administration, Department of Commerce.

Chamber of Commerce

U.S. Chambers of Commerce in both the United States and Mexico can provide comprehensive and up-to-date business information.

Trading Companies

A 1982 U.S. law allows formation of trading companies. For this purpose some provisions of antitrust laws are nullified. Check with your attorney and the International Trade Administration for help in forming and finding trading companies.

Training Programs

Many public and private colleges offer courses on doing business in Mexico. An excellent example is the Small Business Development and International Trade Center in Chula Vista, California. This adjunct of Southwestern College, supported by a variety of public and private organizations, offers a very wide range of services extending from involvement in a MEXUS Post-NAFTA business degree program accredited by San Diego State University and several Mexican universities to practical help in establishing a business in Mexico. It is a sterling example of academic-commercial cooperation.

Relocation and Orientation Companies

Many relocation companies offer cultural as well as moving services. International Orientation Services of Northbrook, Illinois, has one of the best staffs in the business. These companies can arrange housing and schools for children of expatriates in Mexico.

Shelter Companies

Many shelter companies are located along our long border with Mexico. These offer a wide range of services: feasibility studies, establishment of *maquiladoras*, janitorial services for Mexican plants, payroll and medical services for Mexican employees. Cal Pacifico of Newport Beach, California, and TraTec of Chula Vista, California are excellent examples of shelter companies.

Accounting Firms

Most U.S. major accounting firms have offices in Mexico. These companies provide a wide range of services which extend beyond accounting. Price Waterhouse, for example, maintains almost a dozen offices in Mexico.

MEXICAN ORGANIZATIONS

Mexican Embassy and Consulates

The Mexican Embassy and Consulates in the United Slates can be good places to establish contacts for your Mexican venture.

Ministry of Commerce and Industrial Development

The Mexican Ministry of Commerce and Industrial Development is a key agency for Mexican business and should be contacted early in your process of developing business in Mexico.

Private Mexican Organizations

Private Mexican Organizations can be very helpful. These include Comité Empresarial Mexicano para Asuntos Internacionales (CEMAI) and the Mexican Investment Board.

PART THREE

The Personal Experience

This book is not intended to be a tourist guide but this section should help you do business in Mexico. Your business effectiveness will largely depend upon how well you adjust. There will be considerable overlap between your personal and business activities.

You will need diversions from work for relaxation and comic relief. Try to get off the beaten path covered in guide books so you can structure your breaks to increase your understanding of Mexico.

10. Travel Tips

Passports and Visas

Proof of citizenship and photo identification are required for entry to Mexico by U.S. citizens. Except for short visits to border areas tourists should obtain tourist cards. Business visitors should possess U.S. passports with Mexican business visas even for short visits across the border. Some U.S. business people entering Mexican border cities for short visits to their Mexican companies have been fined a thousand dollars for failure to obtain Mexican business visas. Both tourist cards and visas should be validated at Mexican border immigration offices. Apply for these documents at a Mexican embassy or consulate.

There are two types of business visas depending upon whether the recipient will receive direct compensation in Mexico. If renumeration will be received in Mexico, the application could take several months to process.

If you are planning to live in Mexico and do business there, you must request a permit from the Department of Immigration, Av. Chapultepec #284, Esc. Glorieta Insurgentes, Colonia Roma, Mexico, D.F. 06700. The shelter and relocation companies listed in chapter thirteen can help for business moves. Mexican consulates can advise on recent rule changes.

It is best to carry a passport even when the Mexican government does not require it. It may be required as identification at banks, hotels, and currency exchanges. A passport can be helpful in dealing with Mexican authorities. If registered with the U.S. Embassy, it can be quickly replaced if lost.

Timing the Visit

For comfort winter is usually best. Both coasts are hot and humid south of the tropic of Cancer which cuts across Mexico near Mazatlán. Inland elevations are high, producing dryer, cooler climates. On the northern plateau it sometimes freezes. In most parts of Mexico it is hot and wet from May to October, cool and dry from December to February. Baja has seasonal rains from January through March. If your business allows flexibility, visit in November, my favorite choice.

Packing

Since Mexican business dress is more formal than ours, pack a few of your best suits and accessories. Suits are standard for dinner in better restaurants. During the rainy season carry an umbrella and rain coat. For upland areas pack a topcoat and sweaters. If you have a tight itinerary pack a set of drip-dry clothes.

When not doing business plan to dress informally but conservatively: pressed slacks, pleated *guayabera* shirts, tasteful dresses. You will need a hat, sun block, and sunglasses for sun protection; long-sleeved shirts for malaria mosquitoes. Tank tops, sandals, and shorts are suitable for tourist beaches but not churches and traditional communities.

Most toiletries are available in Mexico but bring such items as deodorants, tampons, lip balm, contact lens solution, a sewing kit, diarrhea and cold pills. Prescription medicines should be kept in original vials. Mexican medication control laws are different from ours. Possession of excessive quantities of a drug like Valium can mean arrest if abuse is suspected. Mexico follows Napoleonic law, guilty until proven innocent. Prison terms are long.

If you plan to ride Mexican trains or buses or visit local hotels you need to take items seldom needed in the United States: a plastic flask for water, collapsible cup, hand towel, can opener, small supplies of food and toilet tissue, water purification tablets, insecticides, envelopes and tape (to wrap valuables for hotel safes), a safety razor, flashlight, and batteries for power outages, a neck pouch and money belt.

Arrival

At your point of entry into Mexico be sure to have your visa or tourist card validated by Immigration. Minors without valid passports require notarized consent forms from parent(s) when entering with one parent, alone, or in custody of a non-parent adult.

Current Mexican regulations limit the value of goods brought into Mexico by air or sea to three hundred dollars per person; by land, fifty dollars. Goods exceeding these may be taxed. Exemptions are allowed for fifty cigars, a carton of cigarettes, 250 grams of tobacco, and a camera or camrecorder.

Mexico strictly controls the entry of vehicles. Be sure to bring your registration, driver's license, and obtain Mexican auto insurance. Your U.S. auto insurance will not be valid in Mexico. A permit from a Mexican consulate is required to import guns or ammunition into Mexico, even if the firearm is registered in the United States.

If you are moving to Mexico for a long business assignment, you should seek the help of Mexican Customs, a customs broker, or a shelter or relocation company.

Mexican Customs can be tough. An electronics executive from Philadelphia told me he was grilled at the airport in Mexico City by a customs agent who asked five times why he had possession of two hundred company brochures. Each time his answer was the same, "Because two hundred people are attending the seminar."

Money

Major U.S. credit cards are accepted by many Mexican businesses. Since credit card companies convert pesos to dollars wholesale, your card charges will often get the best rate. The next best, in order of value, will usually be Mexican banks, *casas de cambio* (currency exchanges), and hotels. Due to the steady devaluation of the peso, you should probably keep your money in dollars.

The New Peso, worth one thousand old pesos, was established on January 1, 1993. In transactions the New Peso is listed as "N$."

Traveler's checks are widely honored in Mexico. Cash machines are available at many airports and banks.

Tips are expected for most services including "car watchers" who will vandalize your car if you do not pay them. Keep a supply of small notes and bills for this purpose. U.S. coins are appreciated. Tipping in top hotels and restaurants conforms with U.S. standards. In small local establishments it is not expected.

If your company has you on a tight budget, costs can be minimized in many ways. Good standard rooms in hotels catering to Mexican business people can be obtained at roughly half the U.S. cost. Except in the tourist season rates are negotiable. Transportation and food costs are reasonable. Though imported alcoholic beverages are expensive, Mexican beer is excellent and cheap. Germans taught them how to brew it. Top grades of tequila and rum are smooth, mellow, and inexpensive. Be sure to ask if IVA, Mexico's value-added tax, is included in your bills. Some high-priced purchases, such as air tickets, may list it separately. It should not be added afterwards.

Time

Most of Mexico is in U.S. Central Standard Time. The states of Sonora, Sinaloa, Baja Sur and Nayarit follow Mountain Time. Baja Norte is on U.S. Pacific Time. It follows the U.S. state of California during daylight-saving time.

Getting Around

Aeromexico, Mexican Airlines, and others provide domestic service. Most have open seating. Expect long delays, a long line to buy tickets, and another long line to check baggage.

Travel below first class on Mexican trains and buses can be hellish. Be sure you have reservations for both the vehicle/car and seat/compartment. Trains are usually more comfortable than buses but they move more slowly in mountains. Sleeping compartments provide convenient rest. Fares are cheap.

Buses vary from first class, air-conditioned vehicles with pretty stewardesses, reserved seats, and rest rooms to dilapidated school buses sold to Mexico because they failed U.S. safety tests.

For a short visit to Mexico it is probably best not to drive. Taxis are not expensive. Settle the approximate fee before getting in the cab.

Safety

Mexico is not a paragon of safety. Street crime is common. Murders abound on the highways of Sinaloa, even by day. The U.S. Embassy advises its employees not to travel on Mexican roads after dark. Criminals sometimes represent themselves as police in order to obtain "fines" for framed "crimes." I lock my luggage, not to prevent theft, but to prevent something from being placed *in* it.

In states such as Chiapas there are three kinds of road blocks: army or police blocks to capture rebels, rebel actions to kill government officials, and traditional holdups by classical bandits bent on robbery.

Mexico is losing stability. Revolution ferments in some areas. Political violence is increasing. There are good profits to be made but you must be prepared to protect yourself. Doing business in Mexico involves personal as well as business risks.

To protect yourself from crime leave your valuables in the hotel safe. Use neck or belt pouches for the money you carry. Do not leave valuables visible in your car. Be careful at night and in areas where there are few people. To avoid becoming a hostage for extortion vary your daily schedule and routes. At a stop leave sufficient room in front of your car to allow you to leave the lane quickly. Rent or lease a car with a phone.

Be aware of the potential for political violence by calling the U.S. State Department at (202) 647-5225 for current travel warnings. Stay away from demonstrations. If trapped in one, avoid abrupt moves which either the police or rioters might consider threatening. Do not carry a firearm. In a revolution or civil disturbance it can result in summary execution.

If you anticipate danger obtain a good city map and mark alternate routes from your hotel to your business or negotiating site, airport, police station, U.S. consulate, and other key points. Prepare yourself for a quick departure from Mexico by keeping ready access to your passport, credit cards, return tickets, and some hard currency (pesos could become worthless). Keep some cash in small bills.

Since turmoil might prevent your departure, be prepared to turn your hotel, office, or home into a haven by stocking it with food, drinking water, battery-operated short-wave radio, cellular phone, and local clothing suitable for a disguise.

Return to United States

When you return to the United States, Customs will allow four hundred dollars duty-free. If you have been outside the U.S. more than thirty-one days this is increased. Beyond this regulations are complicated. It is best to contact the U.S. Customs Service, (202) 566-8195, before departing if you plan to bring much back. The Customs Service is somewhat lenient on Mexican goods since Mexico is a developing nation. U.S. border states have strict rules concerning imports of alcohol, tobacco, and perfume.

11. Living in Mexico

Moving and Arrival

Your move to Mexico will be a major project. Many American firms hire relocation companies to process travel documents, find housing, and arrange school enrollment for children. A good relocation company can save more than it costs.

Do not pack items for shipment which you will need during your trip or while awaiting arrival of your goods. While you are settling your finances, save some time to check your car, health and house insurance, and cancel utilities.

Cultural Shock

You will suffer cultural shock when you realize you are not in Mexico as a tourist but as someone who has to live as a foreigner in a strange environment. As soon as your initial enthusiasm for everything Mexican wears off, you will feel frustration and irritation due to difficulties with foreign food, customs, language, and manners. Some expatriates simply give up and go home.

Your business success will depend largely on your personal adjustment. If you avoid cultural shock by staying in a gringo environment, you will have limited business effectiveness. So break out of your shell and learn about Mexico. If you do not speak Spanish buy a phrase book. Ability to ask the cost of an item or location of a restaurant will help. By enrolling in a Spanish course, you can increase your business effectiveness, overcome cultural shock, and open yourself to a rich Mexican heritage. It is easier to learn a language when you are surrounded by it. It can also be fun!

About 350,000 U.S. citizens live in Mexico. Most live well. Though there are large U.S. communities in Tijuana, Guadalajara, Juárez, Lake Chapala, and Monterrey, the largest U.S. business community is in Mexico City, the largest city in the world with a single urban center. Here live some twenty million Mexicans, one of every four, driving three million vehicles, and working in one hundred thousand factories. If you are from New York City or Los Angeles, the traffic congestion and air pollution will help you overcome cultural shock. You will feel at home.

Housing and Schools

Compared to the United States, house rentals are higher in big cities and lower in small towns. Many top-of-the-line houses and apartments in Mexico City rent for $2,500 to $4,000 per month. Utilities, pools, servants, and security guards are often included in these rents. The cheapest apartments suitable for U.S. business people rent for about $1500 per month. Below that accommodations are at the Mexican standard. These could be suitable if investigated carefully. Be sure to check the heating, water, cooking, and electrical systems. Unless you are fluent in Spanish, bring an interpreter on your house hunt. Mexicans call people who speak Spanish poorly *gringos*, meaning "its Greek to me!"

Many of the major cities in Mexico have private elementary and high schools based on the U.S. system. Tuition fees are usually higher than in the United States.

Servants

Most U.S. business expatriates in Mexico employ one or more servants as maids, cooks, gardeners, or drivers. Some are part-time. Probably the best way to obtain a household servant is from another business expatriate who is returning to the United States. Then you will likely have an employee who is honest, reliable, and trained. Though servants are cheap, details such as salary reviews, hours, bonuses, health exams, room and board, holidays, vacations, and termination pay should be settled at the time of hiring. People from the U.S. usually have no experience with servants. They tend to be either too familiar or too authoritarian. For some having servants underfoot all the time can be an invasion of privacy.

Electricity

Current and connections are the same as in the United States: 110 volts, 60 cycle, plugs with two flat prongs. Outages are more frequent in Mexico. Costs of appliances in Mexico are high. You can bring your own washer, dryer, and dishwasher or rely on servants. If you plan to live at higher elevations, such as Guadalajara or Cuernavaca, bring an electric blanket.

Radio, Television, Newspapers

The News is Mexico City's English language daily. Many U.S. newspapers and magazines are available in the larger cities. U.S. television networks are watched in many places through cable and satellite.

Telephone and Mail

Installation of a telephone used to cost over a thousand dollars. With privatization costs are coming down and service is improving. Mexico is rapidly developing a modern telephone system. Offices with phone and FAX are available on short-term rents. Ladatel phone centers are easy, fast, and cheap. Some take credit cards.

Unfortunately mail service is still archaic. It took more than three weeks for my air mail from Mexico to arrive in the United States. For speedy delivery use UPS or Federal Express.

Driving

You will need to obtain an import permit to bring your car into Mexico, but your U.S. driver's license is valid. Be sure to obtain Mexican auto insurance; U.S. auto insurance is not honored in Mexico. Mexican law does not recognize the concept of a car "accident." Even with Mexican insurance you will be taken into police custody until financial and criminal responsibilities are determined. Without Mexican insurance, expect a long stay in jail. Mexican insurance is not valid if the driver is under the influence of drugs or alcohol. It does not cover loss of personal items from cars or theft of *parts* of cars.

Gas stations through Mexico charge the same prices because they are all government owned. *Nova* (regular) gas is leaded and *sin plomo* is unleaded. Using leaded gas in a car designed for unleaded can damage a catalytic converter. Mexican gas is poor in quality; some drivers use an octane enhancer.

Roads vary in quality and can be dangerous at night when livestock and banditos suddenly appear. A fleet of mechanics in green trucks, called (you guessed it) the Green Angels, patrol some highways to help motorists in trouble. Mexico City has daily restrictions on driving based on the last digits of license plates.

Learn the international road signs; they are used in Mexico. Mexican signals can be confusing. If the car ahead of you has a blinking left turn indicator it can be an invitation for you to pass or a signal for a left turn. At narrow bridges or street intersections the first vehicle to flash its lights and honk has the right of way.

Rental cars are available in larger cities. Before leaving the lot be sure to check insurance, condition of car, gas required, and spare tire. Rental agencies in U.S. border towns usually do not allow renters to take cars into Mexico.

Health Problems

Turista, sometimes called Montezuma's Revenge, a sordid stomach and bowel ailment, is a part of the culture you will want to miss. You can also do without cholera, giardia, hepatitis, dengue fever, malaria, schistosomiasis, and dozens of other deadly diseases. This will not be easy. The air you breathe will have germ-laden dust. Breathing the air in Mexico City produces a health risk equal to smoking two packs of cigarettes a day.

Before leaving on an extended business assignment to Mexico you should contact your health professional regarding immunizations, health risks, symptoms, prevention, and medicines. Be sure you have health insurance coverage and obtain a list of doctors and hospitals from a U.S. consulate near the area of your work. Take a standard medical kit.

There are some precautions which will help. Except in the best tourist hotels check to be sure your water and ice have been boiled or treated. Avoid uncooked vegetables; fruit drinks and dairy products sold by street venders; rare meat, fish, and shellfish.

Eat food served hot from the pan or oven. Refuse food exposed to flies or left to stand too long without refrigeration. Arrive at buffet meals soon after they start. In hot weather consume sufficient fluids to avoid heatstroke.

Some food items can usually be presumed safe: fruit with skin you remove yourself; anything canned, bottled, or packaged; coffee or tea prepared with boiling water. In travel you need not patronize viand venders; you can buy the ingredients for a safe meal (sandwiches, fruit, beverages) at any grocery. Ask for safe bottled water, *aqua purifica*.

In areas infested with mosquitoes use insecticides and insect repellents; wear light colors, long trousers, long-sleeved shirts; stay inside at dawn and dusk. Avoid using scents such as perfumes and hair sprays.

12. Things to Do, See, and Learn

Dining

Mexican food is delicious. You will enjoy its wide variety of tastes. Meals usually include three staples: *chiles* (a variety of peppers), *tortillas* (corn flour patties cooked on griddles), and *frijoles* (beans). Beyond these staples the cuisine can be quite imaginative. Try *chiles rellenos poblano* (stuffed chili fried and baked after dipping in egg whites), *machocha* (a mixture of meat, eggs, onions, chiles, and cilantro), and *mole* chicken or turkey (using a sauce of chocolate and hot peppers). Mexican *conejo* (rabbit) dishes are tasty and different. Mexican soups are supreme. Try *gazpacho* (chilled vegetable soup) and *sopa de fideos* (my favorite noodle soup). *Ceviche*, raw seafood marinated in lime and garnished with vegetables, is world famous.

Exotic fruits include pomegranates, guava, mango, papaya, and the fruit of cactus and chicle trees. Some Mexican food is *too* exotic. In a remote village in Chiapas I discovered "jumping chili," a concoction produced by adding a handful of worm (moth larvae) infested Mexican jumping beans. It keeps twitching in your stomach.

Mexico's breweries produce fine dark beers and light lagers. Distilleries create many grades of *tequila*, rum, and brandy. Varieties of the maguey plant produce uniquely Mexican liquors such as *aguamiel, pulque, mezcal,* and *tequila.*

Mexicans eat three meals a day: *desayuno* (breakfast), *comida* (heavy lunch) or *almuerzo* (light lunch), and *la cena* (supper). Lunch, usually the heaviest meal, is served in mid-afternoon; supper, in the late evening.

Shopping

Unfortunately, many Mexican handicrafts are giving way to mass production. Mexico is going plastic. O. J. Simpson's face on a fake leather *serape* is not authentically Mexican. Neither are donkeys painted with stripes to look like zebras. These are used as props for street photographers.

There are still some fine handicraft bargains. Look for black unglazed and green glazed pottery; textiles such as *serapes*, sashes, *rebozos* (shawls), and blouses; blown glassware, leather shoes, boots, belts, and jackets; guitars, and furniture. Taxco is Mexico's most famous silver center; Guanajuato specializes in gold. Both crafts display skills honed for centuries.

For truly authentic items consider paper-mâché *piñatas*, paper dolls from Chiapas used in witchcraft, intaglios of gold, silver, and precious stones; and slides of murals painted in color combinations which could only be Mexican.

Spectator Sports

Mexico offers many spectator sports: soccer, bullfights, cockfights, *charreadas* (rodeos), baseball, basketball; bike, dog, and horseracing; and *jai alai*, the Basque game *pelota. Jai alai* is played between two teams of two men each. They strap *cestas*, shallow baskets, to their forearms, which are used to catch and throw a hard ball at incredible speeds. Bets run high.

Mexicans play excellent baseball. I watched a night game between the Culiacán Tomatoes and the Hermosillo Oranges. Both teams had excellent pitching and adroit defenses involving many double plays. They played an exciting inside game with many bunts and stolen bases. Teams are not named after ethnic minorities such as Redskins or Braves.

Television

Mexican television produces programs so good they are exported to the rest of Latin America. It has its share of potboilers but culture is not neglected. I watched Verdi's opera *Attila* on television during prime hours.

Most small villages, no matter how dirt poor, have a community television dish linking them with the outside world. These dishes will ultimately be more revolutionary than all the rebellions in Chiapas and Tabasco.

Participant Activities

Participant activities include golf, tennis, hunting, fishing, surfing, and dancing. Golf courses range from amateur to professional. Courses are usually owned by hotels but nonguests can usually play for a fee.

Dancing is very popular. Much Mexican music is based on the polka which arrived with the French occupation of the mid-nineteenth century.

Mexico's lakes and rivers have abundant bass and trout. Her seaports, such as Cozumel, Acapulco, and Mazatlán, offer some of the best deep-sea fishing. For hiking and camping try Copper Canyon; for surfing, Santa Rosalilita; for horseback riding, San Cristóbal.

Language Study

Mexico has many Spanish-language study programs ranging from a week to a year. Study centers include Guadalajara, Saltillo, Xalapa, Cuernavaca, San Miguel de Allende, and Mexico City. Even small towns offer courses in Spanish, arts, and crafts. Arrangements can be made for room-and-board with Mexican families. This is an excellent way to learn Spanish. Costs are low.

Sightseeing

The ease with which one enters Mexico obscures profound differences in cultures and customs. As a person interested in doing business in Mexico you should probably sightsee off the tourist path. Concentrate on experiences which will help you understand Mexican politics, economics, society, and business. This is what I tried to do.

Cities and Villages

The past still lives in Mexico's sprawling cities and tiny villages. Ixtapalapa, a key Aztec town long before it was incorporated into Mexico City, is an appropriate example. Here, at the beginning of each fifty-two year cycle the Aztecs held their grandest ritual, the New Fire Ceremony. On top of Star Hill, now called *Cerro de la Estrella*, priests ignited kindling on the chest of a sacrificial person. If the fire fed on the fat of the victim, producing a human candle, the future of the universe was guaranteed. In great joy flames from this fire were carried to all points of the empire.

Modern Mexico City incorporates not only Ixtapalapa but its ideals. The city runs on edict. The mayor is appointed by a one-party government which has retained power for over half a century on the basis of more and more sophisticated election fraud and more and more varieties of coercion.

Even remote villages display a mysterious melding of Indian theocracy and Spanish autocracy. The arrangements of church, plaza, palace, and markets are Indian not Spanish. But Spanish padres fashioned a Catholicism that was cleverly syncretic. It assimilated the ancient Indian gods and transformed them into Christian saints represented by statues with Indian and *mestizo* features. The Indian deities were coated with a veneer of Christianity. Their idols were baptized.

Sun, Sea, and Sand

Mexico's beach cities are good places to visit when you want to leave the smog of Mexico City and bask in the sun.

Cancún is a luxurious beach resort which grew out of nothing. After weeks in authentic Mexican locales, the tourists looked strange to me. Veracruz seemed more Mexican. It was here that Cortéz landed and burned his ships to show his troops there could be no retreat. Here the French landed in their conquest of Mexico. From Veracruz General Scott launched his attack on Mexico City, where his Marines fought a battle which added "the halls of Montezuma" to "The Marine Hymn."

Mazatlán is a typical Mexican beach city. Named "The Place of the Deer" by its Spanish founders, it was developed as a port for exporting Mexican gold. Today its gold is in its sunshine, which attracts pale-skinned *gringos*, who sprawl across its eight miles of sandy beaches. Like Acapulco, Mazatlán features fearless divers, who leap hundreds of feet from high cliff towers into churning water washing between dangerous rocks. One of the divers asked if anyone in the crowd wanted to try the dive. I had a cold that day, but I noticed none of the healthy spectators volunteered.

The sea off Mazatlán is filled with marine life: fish, shrimp, snorkellers, and surfers. Few tourists have problems combining the excellent rum with other activities. They rum-fish, rum-surf, and rum-sunbathe. Some skip the sports and concentrate on the rum.

Like most Mexican beach resorts, Mazatlán has too many hotels and restaurants. There is a need for supplementary recreational facilities such as boat-rental marinas, golf courses, tennis courts, bowling alleys, skating rinks, and shopping malls. There are some good business opportunities here.

Guadalajara

Guadalajara is quintessential Mexico, Mexico's most Mexican city. It created *mariachi* music and the famous *Jarabe Tapatio*, the "Mexican Hat Dance." Music fills the air: opera, folk, classical. My hotel elevator sang Puccini arias. Here originated the *sombrero* and the *charreadas*, the Mexican rodeo. Nearby Tequila produces the national drink. Guadalajara is the best place to experience "Mexicaness" because it embodies the soul of Mexico.

The twin towers of Guadalajara's cathedral, built in 1606, probe the sky above the four plazas surrounding it, punctuating Mexico's religious origins.

The Institute Cultural de Cabañas in the Plaza Tapatiá contains murals painted by José Clemente Orozco. Mural painting is an architectural art which must be seen in the original to be appreciated. The melding of murals with the grace of soaring ceilings and circular domes can not be depicted in two-dimensional photographs. The Orozco murals depict the subjugation of the Indians by the Spanish conquerors. On the ceiling of the dome Orozco brushed into life "The Man of Fire," a mystical portrayal of a flying man-god ascending to heaven. The symbolism of this mural has been controversial in Mexican art circles for decades but any novice like me can be overwhelmed by its power and scale.

For a more mundane Guadalajara experience visit the nearby town of Tequila, home of the national drink. Since the seventeenth century Tequila has grown the agave plant from which tequila is distilled. One becomes inebriated by breathing the air.

Some *tequila* is aged like good wine. There is a protocol for drinking it: lick your hand, sprinkle salt on it, lick the salt, suck a slice of lime, gulp a shot of *tequila*. Then: more salt, more lime, more *tequila*. Some brands have a worm in the bottom of the bottle. When you reach it you are expected to drink the worm. By then you don't mind.

Since *tequila* is too strong for many foreigners, Mexican bartenders (who can be quite resourceful) invented the Margarita, which dilutes *tequila* with lime juice, orange liquer, and salt. Sometimes something else is added. In a recent crackdown in Guadalajara, police confiscated 212 bottles of fake "Herradura" *tequila* laced with fatal methanol. The problem was called to their attention when forty-two people died during a *hora feliz*, a happy hour.

A Train Fiesta

One way to get to know Mexicans is to travel with them on extended trips. There is a certain comradeship between fellow passengers which quickly produces friendly exchanges of feelings and opinions. My trip was on *El Pacifico*, a forty-hour train trip from Mexicali to Guadalajara. No sleepers run on this line, only first-class seats. Bring your own water, food, toilet paper, and blanket. Each car had a spigot labelled "potable water" but no Mexicans drew water from it.

Mexicans like fun. The trip quickly devolved into a forty-hour train fiesta, a beer party with songs and laughter. The entire car shared its food and drink, and contributed to the rowdiness. Three new *amigos* performed an inebriated version of Jarabe Tapatio, the "Mexican Hat Dance" in the vestibule, stepping to my hummed mimic of the music. In the United States we all would have been arrested. Or they would have detached the car.

Tongues loosened with alcohol soon cursed the Mexican government with deep intensity. I felt I was in the middle of an incipient revolt. A typical comment: "The government sold most of our industries and borrows billions from foreigners. Yet our lives do not improve. Where did all that money go?"

In northern Sinaloa one of my new *amigos*, looking at rich, watered, but fallow land, said sadly: "Mexico is so rich in resources. Yet it has so many people who want to work out of work. Why aren't these fields farmed? Why aren't these minerals mined? Wealthy patrons prefer to hold raw land rather than pesos." At that moment we passed dozens of railway boxcars parked on spurs, providing primitive shelter for hundreds of poor people.

North of Tepic another new *amigo* pointed out the village where he was born and described the lives of its people. It consisted of a few scattered huts, each with a few agave plants and coconut trees. Though dirt poor the villagers share their food. Hungry outsiders can eat their fruit as long as they do not take any away. When they get money from odd jobs or from relatives in the United States, they spend it on alcohol and poker rather than buying more land or funding a business. They are resigned to lives which will never improve. I asked him who was responsible for this poverty: the villagers or their government? Would government aid be wasted on gambling and alcohol? How can these people expect their government to make big improvements in their lives when they will not avail themselves of opportunities to make small improvements for themselves? Would they take advantage of work and education programs requiring long, disciplined hours or are they locked into a medieval concept of life in which death, in its certainty, mocks all efforts for improvements? Would they want to be involved in a commercialization which absorbs all other values? He had no answers but I think I knew them.

Chiapas

Chiapas, Mexico's poorest state, is its barometer for political violence. If your company is depending on you to ascertain its political risk you should visit Chiapas for an on-the-spot evaluation. The rebellion which erupted from the Lacondón rain forest helped produce a crash in the Mexican peso and stock market which reverberated through world financial markets. Much of Mexico's future will be decided in Chiapas.

Before visiting Chiapas, read about it. The state's history is replete with ancient Mayan mysticism and bloody rebellions. Start with *Popul Vuh: The Mayan Book of the Dawn of Life*, the national epic of the Quiché Maya. Then read Antonio Garcia de Leon's *Resistencia y Utopia* and the six jungle novels of B. Traven, who also wrote *The Treasure of Sierra Madre*.

The Lacandón rain forest of Chiapas is the sacred haunt of ancient Mayan deities who dwell in the ghostly ruins of

Bonampak, Yaxchilán, and Palenque. Chiapas was never tamed by the Spanish conquerors. Guarded by armies of fog-shrouded trees and bands of rebels, it defies intruders. From its primeval depths have sprung uprisings which have blood-ied the province for three hundred years. Estimates of the number who died in the revolt of New Year's Day, 1994, range from 150 to 2,000.

Half the arable land in Chiapas is owned by two per cent of the landowners, wealthy *mestizos* and descendants of Ger-man Nazis who arrived after World War II. The ideals of Mexico's Revolution, "land and liberty," never penetrated Chiapas. As in Central America, White Death Squads, often consisting of army and police, kept the Indians in peonage and poverty, forced to work in the coffee, timber, and cattle industries for $1.50 per day.

The Indians are suppressed by every person with Euro-pean blood. Even the mustaches of *mestizos* put down the Indians who are unable to grow them. Their babies die of enteritis, flu, and pneumonia.

When they tire of living in insect-infested huts, slaving under a scorching sun, and suffering lash, stocks and rape, they escape to the Las Cañadas area bordering Guatemala. In this region of canyons denuded of trees by too many timber harvests, they work the barren soil. On dry, stony, exposed hillsides they grow scraggly crops of tobacco and corn. The small incomes they earn from selling corn, needed to buy soap and cooking oil, are threatened by cheaper U.S. imports under NAFTA. Corn is as holy to the Mayans as rice is to Japanese. The act of growing it is a sacramental tribute to the Mayan gods of maize. The strange corn gods of Iowa and Missouri shame the maize-spirits of Chiapas.

The plainess of life in Chiapas is alleviated only by spe-cial market days. Then there is color everywhere! The market is a mosaic of somersaulting rainbows exploding in the oranges, reds, and greens of tropical fruit. Music ignites the air. Ventriloquists with talking boxes answer questions like disembodied oracles. Chiapan markets and fiestas are bar-

baric, frightening, and strangely attractive. The Indians consider cameras witchcraft. A few years ago a photographer was stoned to death. In Chiapas one quickly becomes addicted to one's adrenaline.

Markets and fiestas were too few and far between to alleviate the agony of Chiapas. On the first day of January 1994, the day that NAFTA went into effect, Chiapas exploded in Mexico's most serious revolt in a generation. The ski-masked leader of the Zapatista rebels, Sub-comandante Marcos, condemned NAFTA as "a death sentence for Mexico's Indians." Five cities in Chiapas were hit simultaneously in an attack which displayed a high level of military planning, control, command, coordination, and organization. These were no simple Indians on the warpath.

In Chiapas one can have an evening's entertainment with a $6.95 ski mask. That night San Cristóbal seemed surreal, closed, constrained, quietly ominous. The lights of San Domingo Church cast a silver penumbra on the cobblestoned street. The bar at Las Gallerias Restaurant was as quiet as a dry Holiday Inn cocktail lounge until I put on my black ski mask. "I was eight and it was Halloween." The next thing I saw through the mask (as I peacefully sipped a Scotch) was a uniformed police officer. He said I had to take off the mask or he would take it off.

My *machismo* answer: "You and who else?" This was meant to imply he was not big enough to force off my mask, one on one. Fortunately, his understanding of English was insufficient to catch my implication.

He then said something in Spanish which I did not understand. The bartender translated: "Señor, you must give up the ski mask, promise not to interview rebel leaders, and leave the bar or you will be hung from your heels and tortured with cattle prods."

It did not take long to hammer out an agreement. I gave the officer my ski mask, promised not to interview rebel leaders and left the bar.

The next day I interviewed rebel *followers*. This was easy to do because a truce was in effect. The rebel leaders had just returned from vacations (possibly on the slopes of Grenoble where they may have used their ski masks for good purposes) and were negotiating with government representatives. There was freedom of movement. Both sides were in town.

I spoke with soldiers of both the Mexican army and the Zapatista forces. They responded well to offers of brandy from my flask. A young rebel, no more than a boy, carried an old Springfield '03 rifle, the first weapon I fired for record as a young Marine. It is known for its extreme accuracy rather than firepower. We both loved the same weapon so we hit it off well. After finishing my flask he invited me to horseback ride with his squad. They obviously wanted good public relations.

My visit was too short for any but intuitive conclusions. These people will die for their cause. They want full independence which the government will never grant. Truces and negotiations will only delay resolution of the conflict.

Only a few of the rebels had modern weapons. Most carried older firearms, which they seemed to handle and maintain better than the Mexican army units I observed. If the Zapatistas should obtain heavier weapons such as anti-tank and helicopter rockets, rifle-propelled grenades, and heavy mortars, they could become a formidable force. The Mexican army's capability of deploying artillery, armor, and motor transport is greatly restricted by the terrain, which is rugged and verdant, favoring infantry.

For the Mexican government in Chiapas "the light at the end of the tunnel" could be an oncoming train!

13. Useful Addresses

This information is designed to help you if you have to visit Mexico on short notice. Only a few examples are listed in each category. Once you arrive in Mexico use the *National Yellow Pages* (English Edition) available in most hotel rooms. Hotels listed here and their associated restaurants are suitable for business.

Business Training Programs

American School of International Management
Glendale, Arizona 85306
Tel: (602) 978-7011

Business Training Institute
Executive Programs - Ste #244
The American University
3301 New Mexico Ave.
Washington, D.C.
Tel: (202) 686-2771

Small Business Develoment and International Trade Center
Southwestern College
900 Otay Lakes Road - Bldg #1600
Chula Vista, Calif. 91910
Tel: (619) 482-6391
Tel: (619) 421-6700 x5319
Fax: (619) 482-6402

Hotels in Mexico

Hotel Nikko Mexico
Campos Elíseos 204
Mexico City
Tel: (5) 203-40-20

María Isabel-Sheraton
Paseo de la Reforma 325
Mexico City
Tel: (5) 211-00-01

Hotel Century
Liverpool 152
Mexico City
Tel: (5) 584-71-11

Best Western La Mesa Inn
Blvd Díaz Ordaz 50
Tijuana
Tel: (66) 81-65-22

Hotel Real Plaza
Carranza 890
San Luis Potosí
Tel: (481) 14-60-55

Hotel Ambassador
Hidalgo and E Carranza
Monterrey
Tel: (83) 42-20-40

Hotel Veracruz
Independencia & Lerdo
Veracruz
Tel: (29) 31-22-33

Hotel Regency Guadalajara
Avenida Lopez Mateos and
Montezuma, Guadalajara
Tel: (36) 622-66-88

Plaza Juárez
Lincoln at Coyoacán
Ciudad Juarez
Tel: (16) 13-13-10

Hotel El Presidente
Alvaro Obregón 249
Matamoros
Tel: (891) 3-94-40

Camino Real
Playa Sábalo
Mazatlán
Tel: (67) 83-11-11

Hotel Posada Diego
5 Febrero 1
San Cristóbal de las Casas
Tel: (967) 8-05-13

Hotel Victoria
Highway 190
Oaxaca
Tel: (951) 5-26-33

Hotel Molino de Agua
Vallarta 130
Puerto Vallarta
Tel: (322) 2-19-07

Mexican Government Agencies

Mexican Embassy
2829 16th St. N.W.
Washington, D.C.
(202) 234-6000
(Also 36 consulates)

Ministry of Commerce
and Development
Alfonso Reyes 30
06170 Mexico D.F.
Tel: (52-5) 511-4654

Private Organizations in Mexico

American Chamber of Commerce
of Mexico
Lucerna No.78 Col. Juárez
06600 Mexico D.F.
Tel: (52-5) 705-0995

American Express
Paseo de la Reforma 234
Mexico City
(5) 533-03-80

Chamber of Commerce of
Mexico City
Paseo de la Reforma 42
Mexico City
(5) 592-26-77 x226

Comité Empresarial Mexicano
para Asuntos Internacionales
Homero 527-7 o.piso
Col. Polanco, 11570 Mexico D.F.
Tel: 531-7319/531-7036

Mexican Investment Board
Reforma 915
11000 Mexico, D.F.
Tel: (525) 202-7804

Price Waterhouse (accounting)
Río de la Plata No. 48
Col. Cuahtémoc 06500
Mexico D.F.
Tel: 211-7883 (Mail) Apartado
Telex-01772579 Postal 1403-06000

Relocation Companies

Clarke Consulting Group
Three Lagoon Drive-Ste #230
Redwood City, CA 94065
(415) 591-8100

International Orientation
Resources
707 Skokie Blvd. #350
Northbrook, IL 60062
(312) 205-0066

Shelter Companies

Cal Pacifico of Calif.
2675 Customhouse Ct.-Ste. C
San Diego, CA 92173-3618
Tel: (619) 661-9001
FAX: (619) 661-9042

TraTec of Calif., Inc.
3648 Main St. - Ste. #100
Chula Vista, CA 91911
Tel: (619) 476-1155
FAX: (619) 476-1176

Trade Organizations in Mexico

Confederacion de Camaras
Nacionales de Comercio
(Confederation of National
Chambers of Commerce)
Balderas No. 144, Piso 3,
06079 Mexico D. F.
Tel: (52-5) 709-1141138

Camara Nacional de Comercio
de la Ciudad de Mexico
(Mexico City National
Chamber of Commerce)
Paseo de la Reforma 42 - 3 piso
06048 Mexico, D.F.
Tel: (52-5) 705-0549

U.S. Government Agencies in Mexico

Benjamin Franklin Library
(U.S. Information Service)
Paseo de la Reforma 295
Mexico City
Tel: (5) 211-00-42

U.S. Trade Center
Liverpool 31, Colonia Juarez
06600 Mexico D.F.
Tel: (52-5) 591-0155

US&FCS/Consulate-General
Avenida Constitucion
411 Poniente
64000 Monterrey
Tel: (52-83) 45-2120

U.S. Embassy to Mexico
Paseo de la Reforma #305
06500 Mexico D.F.
Tel: (52-5) 211-0042
FAX: (52-5) 207-8938
U.S. Address:
P.O. Box 3087
Laredo, TX 780044-3087

US&FCS/Consulate-General
Progreso 175
44100 Guadalajara
Jalisco, Mexico
Tel: (52-36) 25-03-21

U.S. Government Agencies

Agency for International
Development
320 21st St. NW
Washington, D. C. 20523
Tel: (202) 663-1451

Foreign Agricultural Service
U.S. Department of Agriculture
Washington, D. C. 20250-1000
Tel: (202) 447-7115

Department of Commerce
Office for Mexico Room 3314
14th & Constitution Aves NW
Washington, D.C.
Tel: (202) 482-0300/0305/4464

International Law Division
Library of Congress
Washington, D.C. 20540
Tel: (202) 287-5085

International Trade Administration
14th & Constitution Aves.
Washington, D.C. 20230
Tel: (202) 377-2000

Small Business Administration
Office of International Trade
1441 L Street
Washington, D.C. 20416
Tel: (202) 634-1500

14. Additional Reading

————. The *Arthur Andersen North American Business Source Book*. Chicago, IL: Triumph Books, 1994. (Comprehensive reference for Canadian, Mexican, and U. S. markets.)

Binnendijk, Hans. *National Negotiating Styles*. Washington, D.C: Foreign Service Institute, U.S. State Department, 1987.

Fryer, T. Bruce and Faria, Hugo I. *Spanish for the Business Traveler*. New York, NY: Barron's Educational Series, 1994.

Heusinkveld, Paula. *The Mexicans: An Inside View of a Changing Society*. Worthington, Ohio: Renaissance Publications, 1993. (A perceptive account of changes in Mexican society.)

Kras, E. *Modernizing Mexican Management Style*. Las Cruces, NM: Editts . . . Publishing, 1994. (Muchos help for U.S. managers in Mexico.)

Lustig, Nora. *Mexico: The Remaking of an Economy*. Washington, D.C.: The Brookings Institute, 1992. (A penetrating analysis of the remaking of the Mexican economy: goals, methods, successes, failures.)

Machado, Jr., Manuel A. *Centaur of the North*. Austin, Texas: Eakin Press, 1988. (An up-to-date biography of Pancho Villa.)

Manzella, John L. *Opportunity in Mexico: A Small Business Guide*. Washington, D.C.: Free Trade Consultants, 1992. (This helpful publication is a joint product of the Small Business Administration, Service Corps of Retired Executives, and AT&T.)

Montgomery, Tommie Sue (ed.). *Mexico Today*. Philadelphia: Institute for Study of Human Issues, 1982. (A series of enlightening essays on a wide range of topics relating to Mexico.)

Newman, Gray, and Szterenfeld, Anna. *Business International's Guide to Doing Business in Mexico*. New York: McGraw-Hill, 1993. (A practical guide, bursting with information.)

Pastor, Robert A. and Castañada, Jorge G. *Limits to Friendship: The United States and Mexico*. New York: Random House, 1988. (An incisive dialogue between a Mexican and an American specialist which probes the complexities of cooperation and confrontation between the two nations.)

Paz, Octavio. *The Labyrinth of Solitude*. New York: Grove Press, 1985. (A trenchant study of Mexican life by its prize-winning poet and essayist.)

Riding, Alan. *Distant Neighbors: A Portrait of the Mexicans*. New York: Alfred A. Knopf, 1985. (A psychological study of Mexican culture.)

Zamba, Michael. *Living in Mexico*. Lincolnwood, Illinois: Passport Books, 1991. (A useful guide for expatriates in Mexico.)

Index

Global Business Series
from
Jain Publishing Company

Doing Business with Taiwan
ISBN 0-87573-041-8 (paper)
PRICE: $12.95

Doing Business with Korea
ISBN 0-87573-043-4 (paper)
PRICE: $12.95

Doing Business with Singapore
ISBN 0-87573-042-6 (paper)
PRICE: $12.95

Doing Business with Thailand
ISBN 0-87573-044-2 (paper)
PRICE: $12.95

Doing Business with China
ISBN 0-87573-045-0 (paper)
PRICE: $12.95

Doing Business with Mexico
ISBN 0-87573-046-9 (paper)
PRICE: $12.95

ORDER FORM

ORDERED BY:

Name _____

Street _____

_____

City/State/Zip _____

Daytime Phone No. (_____) _____

QTY	TITLE	PRICE EACH	TOTAL AMOUNT

POSTAGE & HANDLING		
	Subtotal	
	California residents add 8.25% sales tax	
$3.00 First Book $0.50 Each Add'l.	Add Postage & Handling	
	UPS-Ground add $5.00 additional	
	GRAND TOTAL	

Make check or money order (U.S. dollars) payable to Jain Publishing Company.

MasterCard   VISA

Card No. _____

Exp. Date _____

Signature _____

Ordering by Mail:

Customers using credit cards need only to fold their completed order form in half, tape or staple the free ends and add the correct postage.

Customers paying by check or money order must use an envelope.

Ordering by Phone or Fax:

Credit card customers can order by calling or faxing their filled out order form as follows:

Jain Publishing Company
Tel (510) 659-8272
Fax (510) 659-0501

Please allow up to four weeks from receipt of order for delivery. Thank you!

Fold Along Dotted Line

Jain Publishing Company
P.O. Box 3523
Fremont, CA 94539

Attn: Order Department